SINGING IN THE DARK

DEENA BOST

SINGING IN THE DARK

Copyright © 2026 by Deena Bost
Published by UNITED HOUSE Publishing
All rights reserved. No portion of this book may be reproduced or shared in any form - electronic, printed, photocopied, recorded, or by any information storage or retrieval system, without prior written permission from the publisher. The use of short quotations is permitted.

Scripture quotations taken from the (NASB®) New American Standard Bible®, Copyright © 1960, 1971, 1977, 1995, 2020 by The Lockman Foundation. Used by permission. All rights reserved. www.Lockman.org

Scripture quotations taken from The Holy Bible, New International Version®, NIV®. Copyright © 1973, 1978, 1984, 2011 by Biblica, Inc. Used with permission of Zondervan. All rights reserved worldwide. www.zondervan.com

ISBN -978-1-952840-89-0
UNITED HOUSE Publishing Clarkston, Michigan
info@unitedhousepublishing.com
www.unitedhousepublishing.com

Author Photograph: Sadie Bost
Interior Design: Talitha McGuinness;
talitha@unitedhousepublishing.com
Printed in the United States of America 2026 - First Edition

SPECIAL SALES:
Most UNITED HOUSE books are available at special quantity discounts when purchased in bulk by corporations, organizations, and special interest groups. For more information, please email orders@unitedhousepublishing.com.

SINGING IN THE DARK

Dedication

*I would like to dedicate this book to my parents, Roy and Marie McRorie. They gave me a beautiful childhood. They raised me in a faith-filled home, filled with love. They raised me on the foundation of Jesus Christ so that even though I went my own way for many years, trudging through some incredibly dark valleys, I eventually returned. They welcomed me back with open arms and loved me through it all. Praise God, I learned how to sing in the dark. Proverbs 22:6 says,
"Train up a child in the way he should go, even when he is old, he will not depart from it."*

Thanks Mom and Dad!

SINGING IN THE DARK

SINGING IN THE DARK

Endorsements

Singing in the Dark reflects eternal hope in the darkest of times. Through real-life experiences, my precious sister in Christ shows how faith, courage and God's presence can sustain us through every trial. Being part of Deena's life for 20 years has been a deep blessing to me. This book carries the same life, strength, and hope I have witnessed firsthand in her life. It is a beautiful reminder that even in the darkness, God gives us a song to sing.
- *Kim Helms, friend/former school nurse, Cabarrus Co. Schools*

As a principal in the school where Deena served as a Behavior Management Technician, I was fortunate enough to witness firsthand the powerful impact she had on those around her. As a talented artist, animal lover, and a professional who can reach the most troubled and trauma-exposed youth, those titles don't adequately capture the way she uses God's gifts to truly be a difference maker in any setting. Her willingness to share these parts of her imperfect and grace-filled journey in *Singing in the Dark* is sure to leave readers in awe of how a powerful faith can lead an individual through challenges that seem to be insurmountable.
- *Kristy Bullock, friend/former principal, Cabarrus Co. Schools*

I have had the privilege to see Deena grow in Christ over the last 20 years. She has a true heart for the Lord and has been an inspiration to me and many others in that time. These stories are an example of how she uses life experiences to grow in Christ and lead others to Him. My prayer is that this book will help others grow in their walk with the Lord and also convict the hearts of those who don't know Him to enter into a relationship with Jesus as their personal Lord and Savior.
- *Darrell Kluttz, friend/Pastor of Tri County Cowboy Church*

SINGING IN THE DARK

*O Lord my God,
when I in awesome wonder...*

SINGING IN THE DARK

SINGING IN THE DARK

Introduction:

Singing in the Dark was never written to actually be published. Each of these short stories came from my own real-life experiences that have impacted my life and my relationship with God. I hope that they will also have an impact on yours. Or maybe that you will look closer at your own experiences and recognize your loving Father, your creator, your master, and your savior. I know that you have experienced your own pain, struggles, and joy in life. Hopefully, these stories will give you some encouragement along the way.

Acts 16, it tells us about Paul and Silas' journeys and how they were unjustly beaten and thrown in prison. Verse 25 says " about midnight Paul and Silas were praying and singing hymns to God and the others were listening to them."

You know, those other prisoners had to know how Paul and Silas ended up there. They had to be asking themselves how these two men could possibly be praising God at a time like this.

Verse 26 goes on to say, " Suddenly there was sucha violent earthquake that the foundations of the prison were shaken. At once all of the prison doors flew open, and everyone's chains came loose."

EVERYONE'S chains came loose!!

My prayer is that someone reading these stories will be freed. Jesus not only saves; He gives us freedom.

SINGING IN THE DARK

Feeding Time

SINGING IN THE DARK

SINGING IN THE DARK

12/8/2016

I wake as usual, just before the alarm, somewhere between 4:50 and 5:00 a.m. Reluctantly, I roll out from under my cozy covers, pulling on sweatpants and a hoodie. Wearing a headlamp, I step out into the misty, cool morning air. The warmth of my bed had all the human comforts my heart desired at that moment, but this next half hour or so is always the very best part of my day. This is my time with my God.

I begin my routine by sliding on my boots and descending the front porch stairs, feeling my achy knees slowly stir to life. I'm already talking to Him. I thank my heavenly Father for allowing me another day. I thank Him for the pain in my knees because I am grateful for the ability to feel even when that feeling is unpleasant. Imagine life without pain; wouldn't it be amazing? Would it? I may become too comfortable, prideful, willful, and not need God.

2 Corinthians 12:7 (NASB) says, "Because of the extraordinary greatness of the revelations, for this reason, to keep me from exalting myself, there was given to me a thorn in the flesh, a messenger of Satan to torment me—

to keep me from exalting myself!" Yes, I am grateful for my pain.

1 Peter 5:10 says, "After you have suffered for a little while, the God of all grace, who called you to His eternal glory in Christ, will Himself perfect, confirm, strengthen, and establish you." Yes! I am grateful for my pain! He made me; He knows I need to feel pain: physical, emotional, and maybe even spiritual pain.

Walking across my front yard, I rejoice and praise Him for His marvelous creation, the true miracle of darkness. Genesis 1:1-2 says, "In the beginning God created the heavens and the earth. And the earth was a formless and desolate emptiness, and darkness was over the surface of the deep, and the Spirit of God was hovering over the surface of the waters." I have come to love the dark, along with pain. I embrace and look forward to it. I remember, as a child, being afraid of the dark and thinking how awesome it would be if it could always be light, sunny, and beautiful. I don't think so anymore. I know now that I would not appreciate the light without the dark. I need the dark. I come to trust Him more when I depend on Him to lead me through the darkness.

I turn on my headlamp, pricking the darkness just enough to see the path directly before me, thinking about that beautiful verse in Psalm 119:105, "Your Word is a lamp to my feet and a light to my path." I am reminded of the importance of reading His Word, studying it, and memorizing it so that I am always in His light. I thank Him for being enough, always. Even when the darkness becomes so overwhelming that I feel it is smothering me, He is always enough to get me where I need to go.

Stepping into the feed room, I gather my buckets and set them out, ready for grain. The fuzzy black barn cat moves like a shadow, darting up onto her perch atop a feed barrel, purring and rubbing against me as I open the tub containing her primary source of sustenance. She does a good job keeping those tiny, pesky rodents with the beady little eyes out of the barn, although I imagine that there are times those varmints aren't as readily available or plentiful. What if we didn't have to toil for our sustenance? What if we just always had all we ever wanted? Wouldn't it be great?

Luke 12:24 (NIV) says, "Consider the ravens: They do not sow or reap, they have no storeroom or barn; yet God feeds them. And how much more valuable are you than the birds!" His Word also says in Psalm 104:23 (NASB), "A person goes out to his work and to his labor until evening."

1 Timothy 5:8 says, "But if anyone does not provide for his own, and especially for those of his household, he has denied the faith and is worse than an unbeliever."

Would it be great to have all you ever *wanted* provided to you?

My Lord provides me with what I *need*. If I always had all that I ever wanted, I'd be that spoiled child that grows to be an entitled, resentful, self-righteous adult when I don't get what I want. I praise the Lord for meeting my needs and not over-indulging me.

With eight horses to feed, I have four barrels all holding different kinds of grain. All of our horses have different needs. Two of the horses are older, in their twenties. One of them only has a few teeth left, and the other is just a hard keeper, a horse that doesn't hold it's weight well. Those two get a senior feed with all the vitamins and minerals they need, and it dissolves in their mouth; they don't even need teeth. Two of the other horses have metabolic issues and get a special feed for that. My daughter has two horses she rides quite often and uses them for competition, so they also get a different feed. One of them, Genesis–the mare, the myth, the legend–has horrible hooves! They're flat, they crack, and they require regular farrier work and supplements added to her feed to help with those ailments.

God also knows all my ailments, from my head to my toes. He can and will provide each of us with exactly what we need. He nurtures us with His love, His Spirit, His people, and His Word.

Matthew 4:4 (NIV) says, "Jesus answered, 'It is written, "Man shall not live by bread alone, but on every word that comes from the mouth of God."'"
John 3:16 (NASB) says, "For God so loved the world that He gave His only Son, so that everyone who believes in Him will not perish, but have eternal life."
Romans 12:5 says, "So we, who are many, are one body in Christ, and individually parts of one another." Verse 10 says, "Be devoted to one another in brotherly love; give preference to one another in honor." You see, all of these things are minerals, vitamins, supplements, nutrients—our sustenance.

Once I have the feed mixed in the correct feed tubs, I thank God for blessing me with a job so I can afford to feed and care for these animals. Now comes one of the most thrilling moments of my day: the call to the horses.

SINGING IN THE DARK

Our farm is forty-eight acres, divided into six pastures that we rotate to provide better grazing, preventing any of them from being overgrazed. Since they're in the back pasture, farthest from the barn, I stand at the door, call their names, and whistle. My quiet morning is quickly interrupted by the thunder of pounding hooves.

Sometimes, though, a little time goes by, and I hear the rustling of leaves or grass as they plod their way toward me. When the pastures are lush, in the early spring, when the new and tender shoots of green emerge from the warming soil, they may not come at all when I call. They may choose to stay wherever they are, content with what they have. I always offer grain because I always want them to come.

I think of the horses in relation to us believers and our Father. In 2 Timothy 1:9 Paul says,"[God] saved us and called us with a holy calling, not according to our works, but according to His own purpose and grace, which was granted to us in Christ Jesus from all eternity." The Father always calls. Maybe we go quickly; perhaps we choose not to go at all, content to stay wherever we are with what we have, although we know that if we go, we will be blessed. Still, He wants us to come to Him.

I get this exhilarating feeling of joy and rush of excitement when I hear that great rumbling of hooves on earth. Imagine how our Father must feel when we come running. When we are obedient, we are rewarded. There are examples of this throughout the Bible.

Genesis 22:18 says, "And in your seed all the nations of the earth will be blessed, because you have obeyed my voice."

John 15:16 says, "You did not choose me, but I chose you and appointed you so that you would go and bear fruit, and that your fruit would remain, so that whatever you ask of the Father in My name He may give to you." Another one is in 1 John 3:21-22, "Beloved, if our heart does not condemn us, we have confidence before God and whatever we ask, we receive from Him, because we keep His commandments and do the things that are pleasing in His sight."

As the horses near the barn, I watch them closely to ensure they are all sound, up on all fours, and moving well. After they are settled, I go over each one, checking to make sure there are no visible signs of injury or illness. They've been out on pasture for the past twelve hours, and horses are notorious for injuring themselves. One morning, I noticed right away that Genesis had injured her eye. We had to call the vet, and, had I not been checking on her daily and treated her quickly, she could have easily lost that eye. Praise God she's healthy and doing well. I always breathe a sigh of relief and say a prayer of thanks when I see that each horse is safe and unharmed. God watches over us that same way.

Psalm 4:8 says, "In peace I will both lie down and sleep, for you alone, Lord, make me dwell in safety."

2 Thessalonians 3:3 says, "But the Lord is faithful, and he will strengthen and protect you from the evil one."

One of the older horses, Ruby, has heel pain. She was diagnosed many years ago and, in more recent years, has retired completely. My farrier keeps Ruby's hooves trimmed and she gets supplements to keep her comfortable and out of pain. These days, Ruby is getting slower. She is usually the last one to the barn. I know the time is coming when I am going to have to make a decision, a dreaded decision. She's been my horse for sixteen years. She taught my children and one of my best friend's daughters how to ride. She is the sweetest-tempered horse I have ever owned, not to mention beautifully built with excellent bloodlines. Her colt, Little Bit, now a gelding, is my current riding horse. I do love that mare! I often talk to my Father, thanking Him for the wonderful years that He has allowed me to have her, and I ask His wisdom and knowledge to understand when it will be time to let her go. I can't bear the thought of her suffering. I pray for His strength and courage to move quickly when that time comes. He entrusts me with these incredible creatures, therefore, I must do what is best for them.

Proverbs 27:23 says, "Know well the condition of your flocks, and pay attention to your herds."

After checking all my horses over once, I enjoy the sound of them crunching on their grain. I sit in one of the few chairs placed in the center of the barn aisle. Sometimes I sit there and simply wait in the dark, singing a song of praise to my Father.

Psalm 96:1-2 says, "Sing to the Lord a new song; sing to the Lord all the earth. Sing to the Lord, bless his name; Proclaim the good news of his salvation from day to day." I sing and take this time to admit to Him my failures and to ask for forgiveness. I make my requests known to Him, and I thank Him for the many blessings He has given. Then,

I simply sit and listen. I think of Scripture I've recently read or a message I've heard. I know this is one way that God talks to me. John 14:1-3 comes to mind where Jesus says, "Do not let your heart be troubled; believe in God, believe also in me. In my Father's house there are many rooms; if that were not so, I would have told you, because I am going there to prepare a place for you? And if I go and prepare a place for you, I am coming again and will take you to Myself, so that where I am, there you also will be." Jesus continues, "If you love me, you will keep my commands. And I will ask the Father, and He will give you another Helper, so that He may be with you forever; the Helper is the Spirit of truth, whom the world cannot receive because it does not see Him or know Him; but you know Him because He remains with you and will be in you" (John 14:15-27). Oh, how I thank God for saving me and for His Holy Spirit living within me. God is so good! Even on those darkest mornings, when there isn't even the tiniest glimmer from a single star, I have eternal hope.

Jeremiah 29:11 says, "For I know the plans I have for you, declares the Lord, plans for prosperity and not for disaster, to give you a future and a hope." I know the light in the darkness!
John 8:12 says, "Then Jesus again spoke to them, saying, 'I am the Light of the world; the one who follows Me will not walk in the darkness, but will have the Light of life.'" I know that He knows me and I am His!
Jeremiah 1:5 says, "Before I formed you in the womb I knew you."
1 Thessalonians 5:17 says, "Pray without ceasing."
Matthew 6:6 says, "But as for you, when you pray, go into your inner room, close the door and pray to your Father,

who is in secret; then your Father, who sees what is done in secret will reward you."

1 Timothy 2:1-4 says, "First of all, then, I urge that requests, prayers, intercession, and thanksgiving be made on behalf of all people, for kings and all who are in authority, so that we may lead a tranquil and quiet life in all godliness and dignity. This is good and acceptable in the sight of God our Savior, who wants all people to be saved and to come to the knowledge of the truth."

I know that my Father knows me and that I am His! I encourage you to take some time out of your day, every day, to spend with God.

5:00 a.m. is my favorite time of the day. Why? Because it is my first waking moments with my Father.

Dear Lord, I praise You for who You are: my Creator, my King, My Savior, My Lord, my Friend. Please, Lord, forgive me when I fail You. Forgive me when I complain, become prideful, or expect too much. God, I ask that You continue to watch over me and my loved ones. I ask that You lead and guide me in the way You would have me go. Lord, I thank You for the pain, the darkness, Your Word, Your light, sustenance, protection, knowledge, and all the many blessings You have given. Please, Lord, I pray that someone may read this and come to know You or draw closer to You. To God be all glory! Amen.

SINGING IN THE DARK

Building Corners

SINGING IN THE DARK

SINGING IN THE DARK

2/26/2017

On this beautiful February morning, the weather is unusually warm, hinting towards the coming of spring. My husband Jamey and I decide to work on our pasture fence. We originally put this fence up about fifteen years ago, and now the posts are beginning to rot and loosen in the ground. If a wind came up and blew a tree over or if a horse ran into it, the fence probably wouldn't stand against it. Over the last few weeks, we have worked on a section of the fence nearest our house, and we only need to finish one more corner to complete that section.

We load our all-terrain vehicle, the Kubota, with supplies and begin the long process of replacing this corner. As I watch Jamey begin working the old posts around, loosening them enough to pull them up out of the ground, I can't help but think of the hard work that went into building this corner and the fifteen years these posts held strong. I wonder if Jamey and I will be here fifteen years from now to replace this corner we are about to build today. I think about the fragility of this life, that there are no promises for tomorrow, and my thoughts turn to my Lord. I begin praising Him for the years that Jamey and I have had together, building this farm, loving one another, and raising our family. I thank Him for this piece of land that He has blessed us with and our physical abilities to work and care for it.

After a little rocking back and forth, wiggling the old posts around, and loosening the dirt holding them in place, the old posts come up. We remove the insulators and clean the holes before setting the new posts. We remove any debris, leaves, and extra dirt, and then we make the holes a little bigger for the new posts to both fit and have room to tamp dirt around them.God works that way in our lives if we allow Him to. He removes debris from our lives, taking it out and replacing it with bigger, better things that make our lives productive and glorifying to Him. This reminds me of when Jesus cleared out the marketplace of evildoers so that it could be used as the place of worship it was intended to be (John 2:13-17). That's exactly what He wishes for us!

I remember Jamey selecting which cedar trees to cut down for the posts, making sure they were straight and had 'good heart.' Depending on where they are sown, some cedar trees may grow and divide into two or more trunks, weakening the tree, or they may grow crooked, bent by wind or sun. This reminds me of Matthew 13 when Jesus tells a story about a farmer sowing seed and, depending on where the seed fell, determined how the plant grew. We must have fertile soil in our lives for those seeds of faith to grow!

In cedar trees, the heart is very important. The heart is the hard red center that takes a very long time to rot away. I don't know of any other kind of tree that has a heart like cedar—that's why it's used for posts. I hope to be like a straight cedar, chosen by God, having Him in my heart, strong and eternal. I must choose wisely where to plant my roots for this to happen.

Colossians 2:6-7 says, "Therefore, as you have received Christ Jesus the Lord, so walk in Him, having been firmly rooted and now being built up in Him and established in your faith, just as you were instructed, and overflowing with gratitude."

We begin to place the chosen posts in the ground. Once they are in the hole, Jamey makes sure they are centered evenly so that we can tamp dirt in all the way around. We begin adding a little dirt at a time, tamping it down with a stick, packing it tight against the post, repeating this process until the two-foot-deep hole is completely filled and the post is firm in the ground, standing strong once the fence wire is pulled tight around it. This process reminds me of how God prepares us when we are obedient to Him–reading His Word, praying, and having fellowship with others. These things represent the dirt tamped down. It holds us securely in place when under the strains of everyday life.

John 10:28-29 (NIV) says, "I give them eternal life, and they shall never perish; no one will snatch them out of my hand. My Father, who has given them to me, is greater than all; no one can snatch them out of my Father's hand."

After placing the posts firmly in the ground, we add the braces. Jamey uses his chainsaw to trim all the knots and small snags off the posts, smoothing and then notching them where the braces will go. He measures and cuts the braces so that they will fit tightly between the posts–so tightly, in fact, he has to hammer them into place. Once in place, He nails them securely to the posts. As I watch this part of the construction, I'm struck by an amazing awareness of the Trinity—the three posts representing God the Father, Son, and Holy Spirit. The strength of the union is remarkable. As Jamey connects the cedar braces to the handpicked posts in a strong ninety-degree angle, the posts packed two feet in the ground, I observe that no animal, no falling trees, no storm nor wind can pull those posts to the ground. In the same way, I know that God, my Father, Jesus Christ, my Savior, and the Holy Spirit, my Comforter will never fail me. No trials, no enemies, no storm of any kind can take down my God.

In 2 Corinthians 1:21-22 (NASB) it says, "Now He who establishes us with you in Christ and anointed us is God, who also sealed us and gave us the Spirit in our hearts as a pledge." That tells me that with Him in my heart, nothing can take me down either.

Philippians 4:13 says, "I can do all things through [Christ] who strengthens me."

Before putting the fence back up, we place cross wires up from the outside of the posts to the center post from top to bottom and then twist a small stick of cedar tightly in the middle to brace the corner even more. Jamey cuts a piece of wire, nailing it with staples to hold it in place, twisting and securing it against the top brace. I notice as he is working that Jamey has blood running down between his fingers. I immediately think of my Savior, my King, the carpenter, Jesus Christ and His blood that covers my sin. Again, the image of three—this time three crosses on a hill—comes to mind. Jesus Christ hangs on that center cross with the two thieves on each side—the ultimate sacrifice. I'm overwhelmed by the significance of those three posts and those three crosses, the sacrifice made for those two thieves and me, and the choice they had to follow Him or not. I thank the Lord for His blood, my salvation, and the freedom He gives to make that choice.

John 3:16 says, "For God so loved the world that He gave His only Son, that whoever believes in Him shall not perish but have eternal life."

After the hammering of the nails and the twisting of the wire, the corner is finished. His work, too, is finished. John 19:30 says, "Therefore when Jesus had received the sour wine, He said, 'It is finished.' And He bowed His head and gave up His spirit."

We don't have to do anything but believe! It's that simple. However, that is only the beginning of the most incredible adventure of our lives which will lead to changes that we can't possibly imagine. Believing brings peace, joy, hope, and so much more.

Finally, Jamey and I replace the insulators and wire, believing that this corner will hold for another fifteen years. Thank God He has promised us more than fifteen years!

John 14:3 says, "And if I go and prepare a place for you, I am coming again and will take you to Myself, so that where I am, there you also will be." These worldly materials, these posts, my body, will all fail and fade away, but the promises and hope I have in Him are forever!

SINGING IN THE DARK

As we plug the fence back in to charge, I think about how I could have been out riding Little Bit or doing a multitude of other, much more enjoyable things today. I think of how I begrudgingly gathered together all the tools and supplies needed for the task at hand this morning, but now I am feeling so incredibly blessed that God would show up here in this most unusual way. I'm reminded of the wonderful life that is contained inside this fence. I witness the awesomeness and beauty of His creation. He has provided these horses for me to enjoy, love, and nurture. Yes, I am grateful for all that He has revealed to me today in the building of a corner.

Oh, Lord Jesus, I thank You for the sacrifice You made for me. Thank You, Holy Spirit, for showing up in the most mundane of tasks to remind me who I am as a child of God. Forgive me, Lord, when I take You and Your many blessings for granted. Please keep me humble and grateful. I love You, Lord. Amen.

Fruits of the Spirit Along the Trail

SINGING IN THE DARK

SINGING IN THE DARK

6/30/2017

It's a rare, cool, June morning. After fixing breakfast for my family, I put on jeans and boots and head for the barn to feed the horses and saddle my gelding, Little Bit. Little Bit and I trot out the drive and across the road where the trails begin. As I enter the wooded trail, my thoughts turn to God. I begin praising Him and thanking Him for this amazing creature under me that has finally become a good, willing, trustworthy horse. We have been through many trials together throughout his ten years of life with me. I raised Little Bit from a foal and trained him myself, so he is very much a reflection of me: the good, the bad, and the ugly! Talking to God on the trail, I thank Him for this place, this beautiful land, and these incredible trails right here. How truly blessed I am!

As I ride along in the quiet still of the morning, I think about the fruit of the Spirit. Galatians 5:22-25 says, "But the fruit of the Spirit is love, joy, peace, patience, kindness, goodness, faithfulness, gentleness, self-control; against such things there is no law. Now those who belong to Christ Jesus crucified the flesh with its passions and desires. If we live by the Spirit, let's follow the Spirit as well." So, I ask myself, do I truly know those fruits of the Spirit? Is my life producing fruit that glorifies my God? How does the fruit appear in my life?

It's not a coincidence that the first fruit is love. The Greek word translated as fruit is karpos, a singular noun which means "fruit, deed, action, result, profit, or gain." The other eight fruits are manifestations of the greatest gift: love. All alone with me along this beautiful section of trail, my horse is behaving wonderfully well. However, just a few short seconds later, a doe jumps up from the undergrowth right by the trail, and my horse lunges sideways, blowing, snorting, and wheeling around, nearly unseating me. My first reaction was to want to jerk him around and scold him for such behavior. Instead, I reach down and place my hand on his neck, attempting to calm him. He was afraid! He didn't realize that the deer jumping up wasn't a mountain lion about to eat him. He needed reassurance; he needed love. God is love, and that's what He does. If we're walking in the Spirit and something 'spooks' us, He is quick to calm and reassure us.

It begins to drizzle, then comes a steadier, heavier rain. Was I disappointed or angry that it rained on this otherwise perfect day to ride? No! Have you ever been out in the middle of the woods when it rains? I'm sure some of you have. Did you notice the incredibly fresh smell and the sounds, the dripping on leaves and limbs? It is beautiful. Peaceful.

I come upon a ditch the landowners had covered with small logs so that four-wheelers could cross, but the logs are too dangerous for a horse whose hooves could slip between them and get stuck. Little Bit and I go around the makeshift bridge and through the ditch, deep and sticky with mud, the kind that horses really don't like walking through. Even in the mire and rain, I have joy! My horse doesn't hesitate to go on through the mud. When I have joy, peace, and patience, he feels it and responds much better than if I'm the opposite.

Not all of my previous trail rides have gone so well. My little yella fella (he's a palomino horse) has tested me many times, giving me plenty of opportunity to develop a long-tempered spirit with steadfast endurance. Being impatient with a horse creates nothing but more issues, if not in that moment, then in the future moment when that problem occurs again.

Little Bit and I arrive at a creek that runs alongside the trail. Once again, my horse spooks, only this time he is much less dramatic. He raises his head, pricking his ears forward, and plants his hooves firmly in the path, letting me know he is going no further until he knows that whatever is ahead won't kill him. I follow his gaze and see a truly unexpected sight. We'd unwittingly snuck up on four otters swimming and splashing in the creek. They are completely unaware that they have an audience as they go about their business moving downstream. We move slowly and quietly along, following the otters and keeping enough distance between us to avoid startling them. My appreciation of God's creation overflows. How good and faithful He is to me. I can only hope that goodness is produced through me by the Holy Spirit, not by any effort of my own.

I am grateful that my horse was obedient enough to be quiet and still, just as we should be quiet and still and listen to our Master. The more we yield to Christ, the more His spiritual fruit will be evident in our lives. Galatians 5:16-

18 says, "But I say, walk by the Spirit, and you will not carry out the desire of the flesh. For the desire of the flesh is against the Spirit, and the Spirit against the flesh; for these are in opposition to one another, in order to keep you from doing whatever you want. But if you are led by the Spirit, you are not under the law." Instead of doing whatever we want or going wherever we choose, we need to let Him lead, just as my horse allows me to guide him.

The trail begins to turn away from the stream with the playful otters, and we come to a particular spot that is flooded with some not-so-peaceful memories. I had been riding along these trails with several friends, my sister-in-law, and my seven-year-old daughter when a quick-moving storm caught us unaware. Lightning struck close by, and the horses jumped. We all dismounted, and my daughter Sadie started to cry. In a not-so-gentle way, I told her to suck it up and then explained that the horses were already frightened and needed us to remain as calm as possible. Later on, my sister-in-law told me that she, too, was about to cry until I scolded Sadie. I think about how faithful my Lord is. He never falters. In our storms, He is our comfort and our strength when we want nothing more than to bolt and run.

Romans 13:14 says, "But put on the Lord Jesus Christ, and make no provision for the flesh in regard to its lusts." Christ's characteristics are the fruits of the Spirit, and we are to put them on. So, I ask myself: What situations cause me to react in a fleshly manner?

As we near the end of our ride, I decide to take a path we haven't used in a while. It's grown wild with briars snagging my legs and low-hanging limbs scratching at my face and arms. A little farther along, the narrow path suddenly opens up, and there, right at arm's length, are the most beautiful, lush blackberries. Vines and vines of berries freshly washed by the rain hang heavy. Oh, how I do love blackberries! I ask Little Bit to stand as I pick a few for a nice treat on the way home. Maybe the fruit that is produced through me from the Father will help to sustain someone or lead them to salvation.

I pray that I may continue my walk in the Spirit, grow in Christ, produce His fruit, and display to others how to do the same.

Ephesians 2:10 says, "For we are His workmanship, created in Christ Jesus for good works, which God prepared beforehand so that we would walk in them." I've come to the conclusion that this trail we're on, this life of faith, has a point of departure with all hope for the journey ahead. Departure begins when we respond to Christ's call to follow Him.

Like Paul, we "press on toward Christ Jesus" (Phil. 3:14). The fruit comes when we are "pressing on," when we are focused on Christ, following Him, which means we are moving, doing, producing, loving. Don't forget that along the trail, there are times to "be still and know" as well.

Now, here's the best part: the point of arrival. The farther we ride down the trail of faith, the greater the anticipation of reaching home. Our heavenly home. Oh, what a day that will be. When we can untack our faithful mount one last time, rub him down, and turn him loose with a pat of praise for a job well done. And to hear those words ourselves: "Well done my good and faithful servant"

(Matthew 25:23). Praise God! Praise Him for His Word, our trail map that we can read and follow as our guide. Praise Him for our example in Christ, and thank Him for His Holy Spirit living in us!

Jesus, You are amazing! Thank You for being such an example of those fruits of the Spirit. Thank You for showing them to me. I ask, Lord, that You forgive me when I am not producing those fruits as I should. Remind me, Lord, convict my heart to always show love, joy, peace, patience, kindness, goodness, faithfulness, gentleness, and self-control. Thank You for Your Word that I can turn to and use as my trail guide. I love you, Lord! Amen.

Attitude of Entitlement

SINGING IN THE DARK

SINGING IN THE DARK

The Lord is my shepherd, I shall not want.
(Psalm 23:1)

I shall not want. What? How is that? Kids these days, even adults (myself included sometimes), have such an attitude of entitlement. Want, want, want. Even if we do our best as parents to raise our children to be responsible and appreciative, giving thanks for things given to them and taking care of their belongings as well as things that may not belong to them (even more so than their own things!) is difficult to do in this world of, "Give me," "If it's free, it's for me," or even worse than that– the "I deserve it" and, "You owe me" mentality. Take a look around when you go to the shopping mall, watch TV, or even listen to the radio. Advertisements and commercials make us think that we deserve one thing or another. How have we gotten to this place where we feel that we should just be given anything we want? David said that "the Lord is his shepherd, he shall not want." The psalmist then proceeds to tell us what God provides for him and us: green pastures, still waters, protection, rejuvenation, salvation!

My daughter recently had an accident in her newly purchased vehicle, only weeks after getting her driver's license. Now she has a ticket, a court appearance, and costs to repair her car. My husband and I have decided that she will have to work to pay for both her ticket and car repairs. Why? We bought the car for her with the understanding that she would now have the responsibility of caring for it.

Isn't that what Paul meant when he said in Philippians 2:12, "So then, my beloved, just as you have always obeyed, not as in my presence only, but now much more in my absence, work out your own salvation with fear and trembling"? As Christians, we are responsible for "working out our own salvation." How do we do that? Jesus did all the work, and now we do our "spiritual service of worship" (Romans 12:1). We follow His example, we love, we teach, we proclaim His Word, and we share it with the rest of the world.

Does that mean that He leaves us all alone? No! He will never leave us or forsake us. Likewise we, as Sadie's parents, will not leave her all alone; I will go with her to court. I will make sure that when she gets a job she can get to work and back. But I am not going to pay for her consequences. Scripture tells us that we don't earn our salvation. Ephesians 2:8-9 says, "For by *grace* you have been saved through faith; and this is *not from yourselves*, it is the *gift* of God; *not a result of works*, so that no one may boast" (emphasis added). Also, 2 Timothy 1:9-10 says that God "saved us and called us with a holy calling, *not according to our works*, but according to *His own purpose* and *grace*" (emphasis added).

I believe that in this time, in this world with its attitude of entitlement, we have lost sight of humility. We have forgotten what price has been paid for us.

So, if salvation is free, why don't more people accept or ask for it? I believe it all goes back to that attitude of entitlement. That lack of humility. That "I deserve, I shouldn't even have to ask" mentality. Or, maybe they don't value salvation. They don't understand what salvation means, they haven't heard the gospel, or they don't understand that they even need saving. Since they don't value it, they don't have a clue what it cost Jesus or what it cost our Father to send His Son to die a horrific death, shedding His blood for our redemption. Maybe some have heard the story, accepted the sacrifice, asked for forgiveness, but then stepped right back out into the world and got swept into the tidal wave of entitlement—that sea of social norms created by a long line of sinners, unbelievers, and Satan.

What can we do? How do we turn the tide? One thing we as Christians *must* do is teach our children gratitude–and we must lead by example, consistently and continually. My husband and I have tried teaching my daughter that if she is going to own horses, she will have to take responsibility for that ownership. She has to work on the fence, clean stalls, clean out the horse trailer, feed them, care for them, and the list goes on. Now, she is learning the responsibility of owning and driving a car and the consequences of accidents and mistakes. She took for granted that mom or dad was always there to drive her where she wanted to go and put gas in the tank and pay the insurance. She wasn't aware of the responsibilities that came with driving. As I think of those things, I pause, thinking of how many times I have taken my salvation for granted–the price my Lord paid for my sin, the blood poured out for me. I have taken for granted things that seemed to come so freely, just as she took for granted things she thought came so freely.

Jesus Christ is the *only* one who has ever been truly entitled. He did not deserve to bear our sins on the cross! Our children and all those we come in contact with need to know what salvation is, where it comes from, and how it is obtained. We must teach them about humility and grace. We must teach them by our actions as well as our words. We must teach them as Paul taught Timothy: "Hold on to the example of sound words which you have heard from me, in the faith and love which are in Christ Jesus. Protect, through the Holy Spirit who dwells in us, the treasure which has been entrusted to you" (2 Timothy 1:13-14).

Oh God, forgive me for all the times, for all the years I took You for granted. Lord Jesus, thank You for the sacrifice that You suffered for my multitude of sin. Thank You for the promises in Your Word that You will never leave me or forsake me. Thank You for those green pastures and still waters, the protection, the rejuvenation, and the salvation! Help me, Lord, to always remember that my salvation wasn't free. Help me bring my restless, entitled heart to the throne of grace and surrender it to You. Give me Your Spirit of rest, that I may be able to share it with others to glorify You. In Jesus name I pray, Amen.

Chasing Rabbits

SINGING IN THE DARK

SINGING IN THE DARK

04/17/18

This morning at 5:00 a.m., as I was feeding the horses, my little dog Chex was terrorizing the barn cats as per his usual routine. Eventually, one of them ran out of the barn and into the pasture, climbing a tree to avoid his harassment. Chex loves chasing anything that will run from him and then barks like crazy once that thing gets in a tree. My dog is a Cojack (a mix between a Corgi and a Jack Russell), so his breeding has him confused between herding and hunting. Bless his little heart!

As Chex chased the barn cats, I reminisced about another chase from my teenage years. I grew up on a farm, but my parents sold half of it when I was about fifteen or sixteen years old. The people that bought the other half of the farm raised Treeing Walker Coonhounds—beautiful dogs! *Treeing* refers to a hound trailing a scent of his quarry until said quarry scurries up a tree for safety, with the hound below, barking vigorously and distinctively, for as long as it takes for the gun-toting hunter to arrive. *Walker* refers to the man, Thomas Walker, who was the pivotal figure in the breed's early development. *Coonhound* refers to a dog specifically bred to "tree" raccoons in particular, and sometimes bigger game. This breed of dog is perfectly suited for tracking and treeing wild raccoons in their natural haunts. These coonhounds are called 'the people's choice' because they are so alert, intelligent, active, courteous, and courageous, with extreme endurance and a desire to perform.

One day, I was outside with my parents, and one of the neighbors' coonhounds came down for a visit. My mother would sometimes give them table scraps, so they frequented our land as often as possible in hopes of a tasty snack. This dog was young, not completely trained, but fully grown and such a pretty boy. We were admiring him when a rabbit appeared from the woods and hopped across our driveway into a large, open field in search of some tender vegetation. The field contained one small pear tree, no more than four or five feet tall, that my father had planted a few years prior to this event. The young coonhound spotted the rabbit and immediately took chase.

The rabbit sprinted into action with the dog close on his heels. As the rabbit ran across the field, it went right underneath the small pear tree and continued its escape to the woods on the other side of the field. The dog, slowly losing ground on the quick little rabbit, reached the pear tree and abruptly stopped. The young dog then raised his nose in the air, letting out the most amazing, spine-tingling coonhound song: "OOOWooowooo!" As we realized what happened, we laughed until we were nearly crying. This poor dog truly thought the quick little rabbit had somehow climbed that tiny pear tree. He was incredibly proud of himself for accomplishing the feat of treeing that hare. He let all around know what he had done–just what he was bred to do. Or so he thought.

As I recollected that wonderful memory, I thought of how easy it is to be just like that coonhound—how easy it is to be deceived, fooled, and tricked into believing that we are doing exactly what we are supposed to be doing.

In his epistle, John warns believers: "Dear friends, do not believe every spirit, but test the spirits to see whether they are from God, because many false prophets have gone into the world" (1 John 4:1, NIV).

As John said, we have to be cautious in what we believe. This world is filled with 'rabbits,' false prophets, and distractions that take our focus off of God and His will for us. What is it that distracts us? Our business, job, family? Social media, television, church? Oh, the list could go on and on.

Also 1 Corinthians 2:14 (NASB) says, "But a natural person does not accept the things of the Spirit of God, for they are foolishness to Him; and he cannot understand them, because they are spiritually discerned." We are of Adam and Eve, who fell. We are flesh, natural man. Just like that beautiful, young, intelligent dog who is the epitome of his breed, reflecting great bloodlines, bred specifically for one thing. He failed. He was tricked. He was chasing a fast, furry creature right past a tree. His instinct told him that the critter should have gone up that tree. How many times have we chased after something that 'felt right?' Stopped where it 'felt right' and failed God miserably? Especially when things happen quickly, such as when that rabbit pops out of the bush and runs under our noses.

Satan sends rabbits, distractions, and lies to get us off track of what we are really supposed to be doing. In John 8:44 (NIV), Jesus says, "You belong to your father, the devil, and you want to carry out your father's desires. He was a murderer from the beginning, not holding to the truth, for there is no truth in him. When he lies, he speaks his native language, for he is a liar and the father of lies."

Satan wants to separate us, get us off track, get us out on our own so that we will fail our Lord, so that we cannot lead others to Jesus. His goal is to destroy as many lives as he possibly can, and he knows all the tricks of the trade.
At school today, a teacher was reading aloud from an article called "Are These Stories True" by Kristen Lewis, from the *Scholastic Scope* magazine. The article describes how we are lied to everyday by social media and false publishing, creating a crisis in our lives and in our country. Rabbits in pear trees.

One paragraph stood out to me:

> *What we read shapes our view of the world. If our minds are filled with misinformation, our sense of what is real can become skewed. Fake news is not new. It has been a problem since the introduction of the printing press in Europe in 1439. In the centuries that followed, outrageous stories preyed upon people's fears about the unknown and their grief after tragedies. There were nail-biting reports of monsters devouring sailors at sea and claims that sinners were to blame for natural disasters.*

SINGING IN THE DARK

Lewis sums up the article with this statement:

As I wrote this article, I kept a quote by TV news anchor Edward R. Murrow (1908-1965) above my desk, "To be persuasive we must be believable; to be believable we must be credible; to be credible we must be truthful." In other words, people will take you seriously only if you care about the truth.

If we fill our minds with this world, misinformation, and lies, then our sense of what is true can become skewed! We will find ourselves believing that rabbits climb pear trees. Fill it with *truth*, fill it with God's promises, fill it with His Word.

A verse that I go to quite frequently is Romans 12:2 (NIV) which says, "Do not conform to the pattern of this world, but be transformed by the renewing of your mind. Then you will be able to test and approve what God's will is–his good, pleasing and perfect will."

I asked myself: "How can I know, that I know, that I know that I am getting the truth?" The answer is easy: Read God's Word! Pray and talk to God. Ask Him to reveal Himself to me. Ask Him to protect me from evil and deception. Pray for discernment. Ask Him into my heart and take the time to develop a relationship with Him. This is exactly what God's Word instructs in James 1:5 (KJV): "If any of you lack wisdom, let him ask of God, that giveth to all men liberally, and upbraideth not; and it shall be given him."

Similarly, Paul says in 1 Corinthians 14:33 (NASB) that "God is not a God of confusion, but of peace. As in all the churches of the saints."

He cannot lie! He does not deceive!

Lewis's article also tells readers how to detect fake news. She suggests asking if the story is well-researched, if the resources are reliable, if the information can be verified, and finally, who published the original story. How ironic is it that the first printed book on that printing press in 1439 was, of all things, the Bible–the truest, most reliable, most researched, most verified story ever written? Written by the one and only God.

Maybe I am not so different from the dogs in my story. Being a born-again Christian but also a fallen sinner, I can get confused sometimes, like my Cojack dog; his natural instincts keep him wondering what he should be doing. Or sometimes I can be like that purebred coonhound who *knows* his purpose without a doubt but still gets tripped up sometimes by the devil's schemes, having me chase those rabbits. Either way, I *know* that I am a child of God, and I *know* the promises He has made to me. I will try every day to avoid temptation and resist evil. I *know* that God is faithful to forgive me when I fail.

I praise You, Father, for who You are, my Lord and King, my Savior, my Protector, my Shield, and my Redeemer. I thank You, Lord, for the examples that You provide to me in the simplest of things, like a coonhound chasing a rabbit. I pray, God, that You forgive me when I fail You. Forgive me when I allow this world and the prince of the air to lead me away from You and Your ever-loving arms. I ask You to give me wisdom and discernment to know when the evil one is trying to separate me out or cause me to become distracted. God, I thank You for Your Word, the Truth that I can go to and rely on when all else fails. Thank You for loving me! Amen.

SINGING IN THE DARK

His Majesty

SINGING IN THE DARK

SINGING IN THE DARK

5/3/18

Have you ever really taken time to ponder the majesty, the power, the strength, and the glory of God? The Creator of *all* things! Here it is, May, springtime, a time of rebirth, growth, and new life. It's easy to recognize the glory of His creation during this time of year, but how about in the middle of winter? Do you notice it or pay much attention to it then?

My mother-in-law owns a small house in Sparta, North Carolina. It's a beautiful place in the Blue Ridge Mountains where my family and I love running away to in the hot summer months for a nice reprieve. When we visit, we enjoy the New River–tubing, canoeing, kayaking, fishing, swimming, wading, or gathering river stones from the cool mountain water. The beauty of those mountains and that river is breathtaking. However, in the seventeen years that I have been married to my husband, not once have I gone to Sparta in the winter. This year, I decided that I was going to change that.

Over spring break, in early April, just before things started blooming at home, I decided to go up to Sparta for a few days to get away. Just me and my little dog, Chex. Wednesday morning, I fed horses, packed up a few things, and headed for the hills.

I noticed as I was making the long winding drive up the mountain that it was really windy. Once I reached the house and unloaded my things, I took Chex up the hill behind the house for a short walk. The wind was *fierce*, the trees bending at its force. Its gusts nearly pushed me along when my back was to it. In that moment, tossed by the wind, I sensed the power of the Lord–a feeling between fear and awe–a surge of adrenaline, nervous butterflies, and light-headedness all swirling together. I wonder if this might be similar to what it will feel like when I stand before Him someday.

I have experienced several similar moments of breathless awe at God's creation. I've watched a humpback whale breach the surf just past the waves. I've heard the thunder of breaking waves while standing in white sand, nothing but God's pure creation in all its glory in sight. I've held my newborn child and seen the perfection in those tiny toes and that perfect button nose. Such a thing can only come from God. There is no drug, no alcohol, no other substance or human being that can give me the overwhelming sense of joy and humility and fear that comes from beholding a God so powerful, He can give breath and take it away.

The reverence that I felt in those moments was so overwhelming that I wonder how I could even stand. How was I still on my feet and not on my knees, bowing in delight at the majesty and greatness of my God, my King? Psalm 33:8 (NASB) says, "Let all the earth fear the Lord; Let all the inhabitants of the world stand in awe of Him." I stood in awe! Psalm 46:10 (NIV) says, "Be still and know that I am God; I will be exalted among the nations, I will be exalted in the earth." In those moments that I described, I couldn't help but be still. I couldn't help but take that precious time and freeze it forever in my mind and heart.

Romans 1:20 (NASB) says, "For since the creation of the world His invisible attributes, that is, His eternal power and divine nature, have been clearly perceived, being understood by what has been made, so that they are without excuse." If we want to experience God in this way–in His majesty, in His power, we need to pay attention to His glory, His creation. Go outside! Go out before the sun comes up, look up at the stars and moon—He created that! Watch the sunset—He created that! We live in an amazing world.

In that ocean, that mighty wind up in the great Blue Ridge Mountains, God is mighty and majestic! In that tiny baby, God is mighty and majestic! I worship Him not only because He is strong but also because He is good. We were made to give Him glory. Jesus said in Luke 19:40 (ESV), "I tell you, if these were quiet, the very stones would cry out." He was telling the Philistines that if the disciples and others did not praise Him, then the stones would. We are to praise Him, and we are what He created to praise Him. The winds, the oceans, and the mountains are His amazing creation, but we are so much more than that.

The word *halal* in the Old Testament is used for worship of such beauty that can make a person lose their mind. It is the root word of "hallelujah," which comes from combining *halal* and *Yahweh* (the name of God). So, I think "hallelujah" may mean "going crazy for God!"

Throughout life and all of my experiences, from the highest of mountain tops to the lowest, deepest valleys, I hope to always remember those 'hallelujah' moments, those times when the majesty and the power of God was so prevalent as if there was no separation from Him of any kind.

I praise You Lord, for Your mighty power! I praise Your majesty in all of creation. God, I thank You for those moments of awe in my life that I can hold onto. I thank You for loving me and giving me an amazing place to live during my short time here on earth. I can't wait until I am with You always and have that feeling all the time! I can only imagine what heaven will be like, in Your presence. I love You, Lord! Amen.

Ebb and Flow

SINGING IN THE DARK

SINGING IN THE DARK

7/18/18

Over the last month or two, my life has consisted of ebbs and flows. What's ebb and flow? The National Oceanic and Atmospheric Administration defines "ebb and flow" as two phases of the tide or any similar movement of water. The "ebb" is the out-going phase, when the tide drains away from the shore, and the "flow" is the incoming phase, when water rises again. Those words are used in a much more figurative way in our everyday life, though.

I often observe that concept in relationships, the attachments and connections being the flow, detachment and disconnections being the ebb. Those moments in a relationship when the connection is so strong that two people finish one another's sentences, they feel lost when they aren't with the other person, and they have an unexplainable love for that person? That's the *flow*. Then the disconnect is the separation–time apart–the moments when two people lose touch or have some miscommunication, argument, or disagreement. There could be any number of reasons for disconnection or distance in a relationship, even in the closest ones. That's the *ebb*.

SINGING IN THE DARK

Sometimes, we can control the ebbs and flows, but there are many times when that tidal shift happens naturally or is beyond our control. I have seen how the relationships in my life can ebb and flow quickly and drastically, including my relationship with my Heavenly Father. However, God does *not* ebb and flow! Scripture tells of God's unchanging nature:

God is not a man, that He would lie, nor a son of man, that He would change His mind. Has He said, and will He not do it? Or has He spoken, and will He not make it good?
(Numbers 23:19, NASB)

Jesus Christ is the same yesterday and today and forever.
(Hebrews 13:8)

Every good thing given and every perfect gift is from above, coming down from the Father of lights, with whom there is no variation or shifting shadow.
(James 1:17)

The Lord does *not* change!

Let me share some of the more recent ebbs and flows in my life. Two friendships from my younger days have resurfaced, one being a guy from high school. As teenagers, we rode horses together and hung out, drinking and partying and making poor choices. I've only seen him a handful of times since high school, yet out of the blue one day, he called me, and our ebb turned into a flow. My husband and I went to visit him one evening and enjoyed catching up. I felt terrible when he told me that he had been-battling cancer. I immediately thought to myself, *I wonder if he knows Jesus?*

I should have prayed right then in my heart, asking God to lead and guide me in my words and actions. Unfortunately, I didn't, and as the evening progressed, an old temptation presented itself and I failed. I failed my Lord, miserably. I failed my husband and my friend. I ebbed away from God and flowed right towards the temptation of drug use and the devils snare. I wasted a moment that I could have used to witness to him. I was disobedient and, therefore, faced the terrible consequences of giving in to temptation.

The next morning, I felt an incredible, inexplicable battle going on in my spirit. It was torturous! I cried, begging and pleading for God to forgive me. I felt as though there was a physical tugging and pulling inside of me that I hope to never experience again. I was so ashamed of my actions. Praise God, He did not let me suffer long. He forgave me and restored my peace.

Several weeks later, the same friend and a relative of mine came over to camp out on our farm for a weekend. I prayed, asking God to prepare me with His armor, to give me His strength and His love. It was the perfect opportunity to redeem myself in Him. The temptation to take part in casual drug use was there again, and the peer pressure was unreal. My friend asked me why I was not partaking, so I told him. The door was wide open for me to testify, and I certainly wasn't going to let it pass me by this time.

I told my dear friend how I had put drugs before God and allowed them to dictate my life for some time. But He convicted my heart to put it down, and I did. I told him how the Lord has blessed my obedience. God does that! God's Word reassures me.

SINGING IN THE DARK

Through these He has granted to us His precious and magnificent promises, so that by them you may become partakers of the divine nature, having escaped the corruption in the world caused on account of lust.
(2 Peter 1:4)

And that they may come to their senses and escape from the snare of the devil, having been held captive by him to do his will.
(2 Timothy 2:26)

No temptation has overtaken you except something common to mankind; and God is faithful, so He will not allow you to be tempted beyond what you are able, but with the temptation will provide the way of escape also, so that you will be able to endure it.
(1 Corinthians 10:13)

He makes a way! I was obedient and the flow returned with my Lord.

About a week later, I connected with another close friend from school. The crazy, ridiculous things we did together were enough to get us thrown in jail or a grave. We were *wild*. We went our separate ways for a period of time, we ebbed, and when we reconnected later, we flowed, and picked right back up where we had left off—wild again! Then once again we disconnected. So, for the last several years we haven't seen each other at all. I remember the last conversation we had when my walk with Jesus was really getting serious. I tried sharing my faith with her, and I'll never forget what she said to me: "Oh, but I know who you really are."

Ouch!

For years I thought about those words. Then we got together for breakfast one morning. I prayed, asking God to give me His words during our time together. Two and a half hours later we had caught up on the highlights of our lives–our families, events, getting old. But the best part was that we talked about God and what He had been up to. She listened and was excited. We planned to get together again, hopefully regularly. I pray that she will come to know "who I really am" in Christ now. Flow.

The day before this breakfast with my friend, I also had a moment that would have typically caused me and my relationship with my daughter and my Lord to ebb. My youngest child and only daughter, Sadie, had gone to the mountains with a few girlfriends under strict orders that no boys were allowed. Well, you can imagine what I learned on day two of this trip—there were boys. I was at church when I learned this information; I wanted to scream and cuss and get in my car and drive the two-hour drive and pick her up. I was furious. I was ebbing, the tide was going out *fast*.

I called her and calmly told her to pack her things and come home, right now. I was thinking of all the things I wanted to say to her and what consequences I could give. My relationship with her and my Lord was ebbing at the same time, because nothing I was thinking would have been productive, at all. Church service started and the message that my Pastor gave related directly to me. Romans 5:20 says, "The Law came in so that the offense would increase; but where sin increased, grace abounded all the more." He spoke of being a "good kid" then making some major mistakes, but being forgiven. He spoke of how God forgives and redeems.

How could he have known what I was struggling with? Sadie's a good kid, she just messed up. How many times have I messed up? I couldn't condone bad behavior, but I certainly couldn't let my anger over it cause me to sin, either. I talked with my friend and spiritual soulmate, Darrell, after church, and I knew he was praying for me. When I got home, I told my husband what had happened. He knew I was upset, as I thought he should be. He then blew my mind, suggesting that I not have any conversation with her when she got home, but to sleep on it and get up in the morning to deal with it. So I did. I prayed for God to give me His love and His mercy and grace. The next morning, I had an amazing talk with Sadie that involved neither screaming nor yelling. We had a conversation, a great one—the best we've had in a long time. Yes, she received consequences, and yes, she apologized and wasn't sassy or rebellious, which is what I normally get when I overreact with anger. Praise God! Flow!

Another recent example of a family relationship that has seen some ebbs and flows is one with my daddy. I admit that I get so busy in life that I fail to spend as much time with my parents as I should. Over the past several months I have seen my dad change. He forgets things he's done his whole life and then has anxiety over it. Last week my dad was diagnosed with dementia. At first, it rocked my world. I am a daddy's girl. Anytime I have had any kind of issue or question, I called my dad. For me, this is a circumstantial ebb and flow. It's a shame that it takes a diagnosis of dementia to make my relationship with my dad flow again. Sometimes we just drift along in life, and oftentimes we need to be reminded to keep the flow going.

Recently, my cousin passed away from a drug overdose. At his funeral, the pastor's words were comforting, but the peace I found came from the Holy Spirit. I could feel its presence flow. As soon as I got home from the funeral, I felt an almost supernatural sense of urgency to get in my car and go over to the arena where my pastor Darrell was just finishing up our summer horse camp for the day. I wasn't sure why I needed to go, but the feeling was overwhelming and urgent. So, I went.

When I got to the end of my road, I recognized a young man in his driveway across the street, walking to his truck. This young man has really been on my heart lately. About a year ago, I had locked my keys in my car at the grocery store and he had helped me. We talked and learned that we were neighbors and then went our separate ways. Anytime we saw one another in passing we'd wave or make small talk.

Several months ago, I heard that he had gotten hooked on drugs and had beaten his wife pretty badly. I couldn't get him off my mind, even asking Darrell to pray for him. When I saw my neighbor walking to his truck, I knew right then, why I had felt that urgency. I pulled across into his driveway and rolled my window down to say hello. I asked how he was and he said, "Considering the circumstances, I guess I am alright." I told him that I wasn't sure what his circumstances were but that he'd been on my mind and that I was praying for him. I invited him to church. I do not know if he will come or if anything in his life will change, but what I do know is that the Holy

Spirit's prompting was no coincidence. My relationship with my God is close–flowing–I was obedient, and I went.

Recently, I went to the mountains for a few days with a group of friends and family. We decided to canoe down the New River on Thursday. In the front canoe, Jamey, Chex, and I entered a rough spot with several large rocks and rapidly flowing water. Just as I thought we'd made it safely through, we veered sideways, hitting a ridge of rock, and tipping the canoe with all of its contents into the swift current. I had a death grip on my dog, my life vest, and my paddle. The current was so strong that it had me pressed against the rock unable to move. I struggled to work my feet out of the wedge, pushing against the current with every little step. Once I got past the rock, though, there was no bottom! Chex and I were swept away, floating down stream. I felt just a moment of fear before thinking, *God's got this!*

Finally, I felt bottom and was able to walk over to the bank to safety. The rest of the group managed to gather all our belongings and retrieve our capsized canoe from the river. Looking back, I think about the flow of that river and the strength of the current. There's no way to go upstream against that tremendous force and power. John 7:38 says,

The one who believes in Me, as the Scripture said, "From his innermost being will flow rivers of living water."

How I pray that my life will be like that current, that flow, so strong in my Lord that I can't resist. And that others might get caught up in it with me. I want to live in that strong current of our mighty God that no pull of the world can take me out of it. We should never just drift along with no course, no path, or we'll find ourselves in a mess, going the wrong way, hitting rocks, flipping over, going under.

In John 15, Jesus says:

> *If you remain in Me, and My words remain in you, ask whatever you wish, and it will be done for you. . . . You did not choose Me, but I chose you, and appointed you that you would go and bear fruit, and that your fruit would remain, so that whatever you ask of the Father in My name He may give to you.*
> (John 15:7, 16)

Jesus chose me! He says if I *abide* in Him and His word in me, then when I ask, He answers. The word *abide* means to accept or act in accordance with a rule, a decision, or recommendation. Synonyms of abide are, "comply with," "obey," "follow," "keep to," and "conform to." I want the flow of my relationship with my heavenly Father to always be as consistent as possible. I know that my circumstances and choices will cause my relationship to ebb and flow, yet I pray that He will help me to abide in Him. I am grateful that He chose me. I know that my obedience equals flow and that my disobedience equals ebb in my relationship with Him.

When I am obedient, I can clearly feel His presence in my life. I hear His voice and have a firm grasp on the peace that only He can provide. When I seek Him and His way, it doesn't matter what the world throws at me or what trials I may face; He is with me as He promised in Isaiah 43:2:

> *When you pass through the waters, I will be with you; And through the rivers, they will not overflow you.*

SINGING IN THE DARK

Praise God!

I love you Lord!

Dear Father, please forgive me when I drift with whatever current seems good at the time. Forgive me when my relationship with you ebbs due to my poor choices or lack of obedience. God, please help me to always abide in You, to always seek You and Your will in my life. I pray that there will be much more flow in my life towards You. Thank You Lord for loving me and always providing me a way. In my precious Savior's name I pray. Amen.

A Season of Change

SINGING IN THE DARK

SINGING IN THE DARK

10/18/18

 The best time of year is when the summer heat dies down and northern breezes begin to blow the cooler air in. I love this season and all that comes with it. Building a fire in our outdoor heater, or enjoying a bonfire after a hard day's work of gathering firewood and clearing pastures of the limbs and trees from the previous storm season.

I long to be outside. I long to ignore the indoor, mundane chores. I would much rather check fence lines and stack hay than wash dishes and do laundry. Crisp, clear mornings hang heavy with dew and the smell of wood smoke as a frantic little squirrel scrambles in search of acorns to sustain him through the upcoming months when the barren landscape no longer bears sustenance. Leaves become a beautiful stained glass canopy of color and lose their grip from their heavenly home, drifting down like fallen angels. Oh, yes, what a glorious time!

This particular season has come with some sadness to our farm. With the ownership of animals comes unimaginable responsibilities. One responsibility is making the decision to let an animal take its final breath. That's probably one of the most important jobs God gives us as stewards of His creation.

I have had the enormous pleasure of owning and caring for some amazing horses in my lifetime but have never had to make that difficult decision until this season. My old mare, Ruby, had reached the time when she was no longer comfortable. She was the last to the barn at feeding time. Her steps were choppy and her breathing labored. She had lost many of her teeth, and even with the best quality soaked feed and mash that I could give her, she was thinning.

When I bought her nineteen years ago, she was such a comfort to me during a difficult time in my life. She was part of many milestones, including my wedding. Her mane had been soaked in my tears more than one time. She taught me many important lessons about life. She was not the easiest horse to ride, which was good for the kids who learned how to ride her. She never bucked or reared but only wanted to be still. She was lazy, and riders had their work cut out for them when it was time to get her going. She loved to nuzzle in people's hair when they stood near. She even foaled a beautiful, golden, goofy colt that I now use as my riding horse. In the last four or five years she had done nothing but adorn our pastures with her beauty and grace. She has lived a good life, and she has earned a peaceful death.

Then there's Charlie, the old man. A big-boned chestnut gelding that belonged to a dear friend of mine. Boarded at our farm for the last ten years or so, he too was experiencing the effects of old age. He had lost much of his muscling across his top line and was thinning as well. He was becoming so arthritic in his neck that he would get stuck with his head down to the ground, unable to lift it. After chiropractic work and supplements began to lose their benefits, I had to call his owner and talk with her about the choice she was going to have to make.

Charlie was an amazingly well-trained boy. He was used predominantly for trail riding by his owner, but she allowed me to use him with my 4-H kids. He carried not only my daughter, but also other kids and adults on the trail and in the ring, during camps and local shows displaying his versatility and steadfastness. He was a gentle, sometimes timid, soul with a loving disposition. He was funny too. If an adult who he sensed knew what they were doing asked him to lope, he would occasionally throw in a little crow hop now and then to keep them on their toes. He was such an obedient creature, always wanting to please. He served well for a long time and earned a dignified departure.

These two elderly equine friends of mine were also friends to one another. There were many days, especially near the end, that I would find the two of them alone together in the barn lot. The other horses would be off in another pasture, but those two stayed together. Many times I noticed that they even grazed together, separate from the rest of the herd out in the pasture. I believe they must have enjoyed each other's company pretty well. So, when I decided that it was time to let Ruby go, it seemed natural to see if Charlie's owner was ready to let him go too. I didn't really know what to expect when I called her. I talked to her often, and she knew that the arthritis was getting worse. Winter months were quickly approaching, and I told her that I wasn't sure how either of them would hold up. She trusted me. She came to visit and then assured me that she too felt it was time.

The decision was not an easy one to make. I loved those animals. God had blessed me with them, and I needed to know I wasn't making a hasty decision. I prayed. I spent time with them. I read Scripture and talked to other friends who had made similar decisions. I didn't want to go out to the pasture one day and find either of them down, unable to get up. I didn't want to wait for pain to destroy the regal air of their character. I chose peace and comfort and love for them. I chose to listen to my Lord, to be obedient, not selfish.

In this season of change and difficult decisions, I have noticed too, the changes in myself. I am trying harder to follow Jesus. In paying more attention to the works of my Savior, works of evil have come to light as well. My sin has taken on new meaning. The conviction is more painful, as it should be. The prayers asking forgiveness come quicker. The redemption is more wonderful, more valuable.

As I age, and the seasons change, I draw comfort from the Master. I know that He cares for me and no matter what trials I face, what temptations I endure or fail, He will pick me up. He will always be with me and has promised that He has a place for me when this life on earth is over. I am finding more joy in my struggles. I know without a doubt that my purpose is to serve Him, in all things. I have found love for the unlovable and forgiveness for the unforgivable. I have the blessed hope found in my Savior, Jesus Christ.

Even in the sad times, I rejoice in this season. Just as the changes in my life happen gradually, as the sun rises and sets slowly, so do the seasons change. It would be harder on us all if we went from blistering heat to bitter cold overnight or darkest of night to brightest of day in an instant. God knew when He made us that we needed the slow change of the seasons in our lives.

Sometimes unexpected tragedies come. He is there for us in those times as well. But for the most part, we know when changes are coming. We know that our loved ones are not going to live forever. In this particular situation, I knew this day would come and had been preparing myself. On the day that we had decided to put the horses down, a nice cool breeze blew. It was the coolest day of the year yet. It was as though God answered my prayer. I needed to feel the cold, I needed to know that change was on the way. The colder temperatures would be here soon, and the achy old bones of those sweet, loyal animals could not stand another hard winter.

I walked those two horses up the hill to the back of our farm, to the most beautiful spot on our property, overlooking the still green pastures, to say my final goodbyes. I stuck my face in their manes one last time and drew in the comforting smell of those warm bodies. I praised God for each of them. I praised Him for thinking me worthy to care for His amazing creation. I cried, overcome with an incredible sense of peace, the peace of the Holy Spirit filling my soul. This season of change has given me a hope and a joy that I never would have had without those two horses and my Father's love.

SINGING IN THE DARK

These Scriptures are God's promises to His children, and where I go when I struggle:

These things I have spoken to you so that in me you may have peace. In the world you have tribulation; but take courage; I have overcome the world.
(John 16:33)

God is our refuge and strength, a very ready help in trouble. Therefore we will not fear, though the earth shakes and the mountains slip into the heart of the sea; though its waters roar and foam, though the mountains quake at its swelling pride.
(Psalm 46:1-3)

Oh Lord, You are the God of our seasons. You are the One who plans the temperature changes, the hills and the valleys. I praise you for those difficult times when I lean in closer and draw on your strength. Please forgive me Father for even trying to do things, anything, without you. Lord, comfort me when times of sorrow become overwhelming. Thank you for your Holy Spirit! Amen.

Scars

SINGING IN THE DARK

SINGING IN THE DARK

2/20/19

On a hot summer day, several years ago, when my family and I were baling hay, I had an accident that left a nice scar on my upper thigh. My husband Jamey was pulling the tractor and trailer loaded with square bales into the aisle of the barn so that we could transfer it into the loft. At the time, we owned several horses and a big Percheron draft mule named Lulu.

Lulu was enjoying the cool of the barn when Jamey interrupted her day. I was standing just outside the barn entrance as he was pulling in. Instead of going out the other side of the barn, Lulu made an exit right where I was standing. A metal pipe connected to our water lines was sticking up out of the ground just beside where I was standing. The pipe had been pinched together at the top leaving sharp points. As Lulu blew past me, she knocked me into this pipe gashing my left leg open. My instinct was to just put my hand on it. The pain wasn't too bad, so I took my hand away, revealing the torn clothing and torn flesh. It didn't bleed very much since it was a flesh wound, but it looked quite deep and long.

Deciding that it really wasn't all that bad, I climbed up onto the trailer to continue working. However, when my husband saw the torn clothing and investigated further, he sent me to the house to clean up while he and my son Cody finished unloading the hay into the barn. I cleaned the gaping wound and patched it up best I could.

The next day I went to see our school nurse who also happened to be my dear friend. When I told her about my incident, she insisted on seeing the wound, scolding me for not going to an urgent care or emergency room for stitches. She cleaned it and applied butterfly bandages, hoping to hold the wound together so that it would heal better without too much of a scar.

Many years later, there is a pretty noticeable scar there, where the tips of my fingers touch my thigh when my arm is relaxed at my side. I feel and see it quite often. It reminds me of that moment. The smell of fresh hay and diesel fuel. That big mule barreling out and toppling me over. The moment of fear at the sight of the wound but then the quick realization that it wasn't as bad as it appeared. This is just one of the many scars I have from living life on a farm my whole life. Like the one on my chin from a young green horse jumping a barbed wire fence with me when I was about seven or eight years old. She didn't clear the fence, causing me and her to both get tangled in the wire leaving both of us with scars. Or the scars on my knees from falling once as a child on a broken bottle during a sack race at church and then as an adult falling on a rock as I was gathering brush up in our pasture. That was a bad one, requiring internal and external stitches and causing great pain for several weeks.

SINGING IN THE DARK

Isn't it funny how we talk about our scars? Everyone seems to have them. Many times, we share the stories of how we got them, bragging or laughing about them. But what about those scars that are just too painful to talk about? Many times, those scars are the ones we can't see, but the memories are just as vivid. Maybe even more so. Sometimes the trauma from those old wounds never leaves us. The invisible scars cause us the most trouble. These are the ones that leave us battered and broken, unable to heal.

I was seven years old when I received the ugliest scar of my life. The farmhouse where I grew up had a long, wooded driveway shaped like a Y. My older brother and I always used one side of the curved Y to reach our home when we got off the school bus. I learned later on that two days prior to the tragic event, our bus driver noticed a strange vehicle that had been parked on the other side of the driveway and wrote its tag number down. On the third day, the strange vehicle was now parked on the side we walked, but the car could not be seen from the road. We couldn't see it until we came around a bend in the drive and it was right there in front of us. As we approached, a man got out of the car, carrying a gun. He threatened to shoot both of us if we made any noise, directing my brother to stand down the driveway just a bit where he could see if anyone was coming from the house. The man then threw me in the ditch, pulled my clothes off, and molested me. I am not sure how much time passed, but I remember crying and screaming even though I was afraid he would kill me or my brother. My brother then yelled, "Someone's coming!" The man jumped up, got in his car, and sped out of the drive.

After that moment, I have no more memory of what happened that day, or even how my parents found out. The only other memory I have is going to court, sitting in the courtroom and finding out that the same man had abducted another girl, taking her away from her home and abusing her just as he had abused me. I remember seeing him sitting with a woman who was crying because this man was going to prison. I remember feeling shame, thinking that she was crying because of something I had done.

That was it. No one ever spoke of that event ever again. My parents never spoke to me about it. My brother and I never spoke of it. It was like it never happened.

Over the years, the memories would resurface from time to time. Those memories were incredibly painful to relive, so I put them away. I covered them up, burying them the best way I could. The worst part about this scar was that I covered it with so much junk. When I was a teenager, I began using drugs and alcohol, which continued for a large part of the next forty years. I was also reckless, having sex with many men, those I knew and those I didn't know. I chose to have relationships with abusive people, and I hurt many along the way. I became angry and emotionally out of control.

For years, I couldn't understand why I made such poor choices. I never realized or acknowledged that I was numbing a pain, putting my hand over a wound–not looking at it for fear of how bad it was.

But God! Here's the good part:

God told Moses and Israel, "I, the Lord, am your healer" (Exodus 15:26).

Paul says, "We are afflicted in every way, but not crushed; perplexed, but not despairing; persecuted, but not abandoned; struck down, but not destroyed" (2 Corinthians 4:8-11).

I gave my life to Jesus Christ several years after this incident. I was baptized and believed that I was saved. However, growing up, I turned my back on God and embraced a life of sin. Now, I have once again made the decision to live for Him. Over the last several years God has really been working in my life, changing me and removing, slowly, gradually, the many layers of sin that I used to cover my wounds. He has placed people in my life who have helped me grow in Him and encourage me and help me to be a true part of the body of Christ. Praise God–He has forgiven me, He has redeemed me and clothed me in His righteousness!

> *"Blessed be the God and the Father of our Lord Jesus Christ, who has blessed us with every spiritual blessing in the heavenly places in Christ, just as He chose us in Him before the foundation of the world, that we would be holy and blameless before Him. In love, he predestined us to adoption as sons and daughters through Jesus Christ."*
> (Ephesians 1:3-5)

My scars are no longer mine! They are His. He took them. I am free!

> *"For all have sinned and fall short of the glory of God, being justified as a gift by His grace through the redemption which is in Christ Jesus."*
> (Romans 3:23-24)

SINGING IN THE DARK

"But he was pierced for our offenses, He was crushed for our wrongdoings; The punishment for our well-being was laid upon Him, And by His wounds we are healed."
(Isaiah 53:5)

This has not been an easy healing process, and I believe that God's timing was everything in this situation.

Several days ago, I was spending time with one of the most amazing people I know. We have grown together in our walk with Christ for the past several years. As we spent time together that day, conversation led to the topic of my molestation. This is not something that happens on a regular basis, in fact–I have only told a few select people in my lifetime. Even just breathing the words of what happened brought a feeling of overbearing shame and incredible pain. However, over the course of this conversation, which I now know God was leading, the healing process began. We talked, we cried, we prayed.

The next day, I taught adult Sunday School, and the lesson was about gifts from God. We read 1 Peter 4:10-11 which says, "As each one has received a special gift, employ it in serving one another as good stewards of the multifaceted grace of God. Whoever speaks is to do so as one who is speaking actual words of God; whoever serves is to do so as one who is serving by the strength which God supplies; so that in all things God may be glorified through Jesus Christ, to whom belongs the glory and dominion forever and ever. Amen."

I immediately began to think of my situation. How could my story possibly become something that I use to glorify

Him? This verse also spoke of using the ability which *God* supplies. Not my ability, not me trying to *fix* things, but *His* strength, *His* ability.

The lesson went on, although interrupted several times with my uncontrollable emotions and tears. We read from the story in Acts when, shortly after Jesus had ascended into heaven and the disciples had received the power of the Holy Spirit, Peter entered the Temple gates where a man crippled from birth sat. He couldn't walk, so his family and friends carried him to the Temple every day, hoping to receive money. He asked Peter and John for money as they entered the Temple. Peter told him, "I have no silver or gold, but what I do have I give to you." No money, only grace. Peter then said to the man, "In the name of Jesus Christ of Nazareth, rise up and walk!" Instantly, grace exploded on the scene! The man began worshiping God as the people watched, amazed.

This parable illustrates how we should use our gifts to glorify God. But for me, the one element of the story that stood out was that the man's friends and family had to carry him to the Temple every day, and that is how he came to be blessed. I immediately thought of my friend, carrying me to the Temple, talking to me, praying for me. I am not sure that I would have ever taken the first step toward healing this wound without that friend, without the Holy Spirit leading his life.

As the day continued, that same friend led the service in tears and read the following Scriptures:

Trust in the Lord with all your heart and lean not on your

*own understanding; In all your ways acknowledge Him,
and He shall direct your paths.*
(Proverbs 3:5-6, NKJV)

Because of the extraordinary greatness of the revelations, for this reason, to keep me from exalting myself, there was given to me a thorn in the flesh, a messenger of Satan to torment me–to keep me from exalting myself! Concerning this I pleaded with the Lord three times that it might leave me. And He said to me, "My grace is sufficient for you, for power is perfected in weakness." Most gladly, therefore, I will rather boast about my weaknesses, so that the power of Christ may dwell in me. Therefore I delight in weaknesses, in insults, in distresses, in persecutions, in difficulties, in behalf of Christ; for when I am weak, then I am strong.
(2 Corinthians 12:7-10)

*No, in all these things we are more than conquerors
through him who loved us.*
(Romans 8:37, NIV)

Blessed be the God and Father of our Lord Jesus Christ, who according to His great mercy has caused us to be born again to a living hope through the resurrection of Jesus Christ from the dead, to obtain an inheritance which is imperishable, undefiled, and will not fade away, reserved in heaven for you, who are protected by the power of God through faith for a salvation ready to be revealed in the last time. In this you greatly rejoice, though now for a little while, if necessary, you have been distressed by various trials, so that the proof of your faith, being more precious than gold which perishes though tested by fire, may be

found to result in praise, glory, and honor at the revelation of Jesus Christ; and though you have not seen Him, you love Him, and though you do not see Him now, but believe in Him, you greatly rejoice with joy inexpressible and full of glory, obtaining as the outcome of your faith, the salvation of your souls. As to this salvation, the prophets who prophesied of the grace that would come to you made careful searches and inquiries.
(1 Peter 1:3-10)

Wow. I cried with him as he read these verses! I knew healing was coming; I knew that I would glorify God in all things, even the most horrible act that has ever been committed against me.

So, today, as I write this, I am healing. I know that it takes time and I know that the devil will try to use all that he has to cause me to stumble. The spiritual battle that has been raging in my mind has been so incredible at times that I wanted to shut it all down. I wanted to hate the people who care about me. I wanted to turn my back on God once again. The pain has been unreal. But through Scripture, prayer, friendship, and spiritual prayer warriors, I have managed to keep going.

I know that I will continue to struggle with my emotions, my anger, as well as the old temptations of my sin. I know that I will have to continue to work on forgiving myself and fully trusting Him. But, I know that my God is greater and that He is the ultimate healer. I refuse to cover the wound any longer. It is open and He is pouring out soothing ointment!

In Mark 5, Jesus heals a woman who has been afflicted for many years. Her faith is strong, and she knows that if she only touches his garment, she will be made well. Jesus says to her, "Daughter, your faith has made you well. Go in peace, and be healed of your affliction."

Hebrews 11: 6 says, "And without faith it is impossible to please Him, for the one who comes to God must believe that He exists, and that He proves to be One who rewards those who seek Him."

My faith has been tested in this, but is now stronger than ever!

Now I will do all that I can to focus on His scars, not mine. Thomas refused to believe until Jesus told him to put his hands in the scars. In John: 20:29 Jesus told him: "Because you have seen me, have you now believed? Blessed are they who did not see, and yet believed."

Oh, I believe!

Just as the scars we can't see seem to hurt us the most, the Healer, the one we can't see, can heal them as long as we believe.

When a certain smell or thought or word triggers memories, making the scars become real again, just like those that I can feel under my fingertips cause me to remember the day that my mule sent me tumbling, I will think of Him. I will remember what He did on that tree for me, so I can be free.

I will diligently seek Him. I will stay in His Word. I will

SINGING IN THE DARK

fellowship with my brothers and sisters who are praying for me and are willing to carry me when I can't walk. I will glorify God in all things! And I will use my scars to serve others.

I love these verses in Isaiah 61, and I will finish with them:
The Spirit of the Lord God is upon me,
Because the Lord anointed me
To bring good news to the humble;
He has sent me to bind up the brokenhearted,
To proclaim release to captives
And freedom to prisoners;
To proclaim the favorable year of the Lord.
And the day of vengeance of our God;
To comfort all who mourn,
To grant those who mourn in Zion,
Giving them a garland instead of ashes,
The oil of gladness instead of mourning,
The cloak of praise instead of a disheartened spirit.
So they will be called oaks of righteousness,
The planting of the Lord, that He may be glorified.
(Isaiah 61:1-3)

Lord, I love you! I thank you God for your mercy and grace! Amen.

SINGING IN THE DARK

Trail Riding

SINGING IN THE DARK

SINGING IN THE DARK

3/13/2019

    Trail riding is my favorite pastime. This winter has been so wet and nasty that it has been nearly impossible to get out on the trails, or at least the trails that I like to ride. Sure I could haul my horse to a location that has wide, flat, easy trails, and I probably would if you didn't have to pay ten dollars to ride there, but riding around in my own pastures is better than doing that. You see, I have *this thing* and I have passed *this thing* along to my daughter as well. *This* is the *thing*: easy trails are *incredibly* boring. I long for adventure–challenging trails, something with obstacles like scary steep hills, streams, rivers, logs to cross over, switchbacks in the trail, and narrow trails on the sides of mountains are what I enjoy. Trailblazing is even better. There is something about being out in the middle of nowhere, no trail, no sign of human life, that is humbling and exhilarating all at the same time. I have found myself lost a time or two, especially with one particular friend of mine who always seems to get turned around when leading the way. Of course that friend claims that we have never been *truly* lost. I really don't mind getting lost, as long as we have plenty of time to find our way back to a trail before dark. Then there are those intentional night rides that I have had the pleasure to endeavor. Now those are fun! I wait until there is a full moon and then saddle up and head out, letting the moon light the way. That feat will separate the bold from the timid rider for sure.

There have been quite a few people who have gone on trail rides with me over the span of my life. Some have loved the adventure as I do, while others have never returned to ride with me again. I would never intentionally put a horse or rider in any kind of situation where they could get seriously injured. However, it must be understood that anytime you ride a horse, whether in a nice sandy round pen, or on one of those trails hanging on the side of a cliff, and whether it is on the most highly trained or the greenest, barely-trained horse, there is always the danger of someone getting hurt–horse and/or rider. In the past I have wrongly assumed that those riding with me are just as eager to experience life on the trail to its fullest as I am.

The years spent on the trail have taught me many things. I have learned to check beforehand with those I am with to find out if they are truly experienced and ready for anything a ride could bring. I have learned to make sure that if the trail I am going on is very challenging, that I must have a horse that is also up for the challenge, physically and mentally. When I am miles away from the trailhead and the horse shuts down due to physical exhaustion, that is never a good thing. Or, when I am miles away from home and the horse dumps me and high tails it home without me, that too can lead to physical exhaustion, this time my own. Those moments can lead to spiritual and emotional exhaustion as well. I sometimes wonder how many good horses have been sold because of that sort of experience. I understand it all too well. I have learned to be prepared. If it's a short ride on familiar trails, saddle bags may be unnecessary. If it's a long ride on unfamiliar trails, then saddle bags loaded with food, drink, first aid, etc. are a necessity.

If it came to it, which path would you take? How would you prepare? Would you take the path less traveled? The one that looks a little narrow, like a deer trail through the bushes, where you can't see much farther than in front of your horses' nose? Or how about the one that is wide and clear, with nice dry footing and without a single branch in the way. Would you head out at the break of dawn, with a full day ahead and plenty of daylight to burn in order to be back home well before dusk? Or do you like to take that moonlight ride, trusting your horses' steps and enjoying the completely different awakening of the senses that sort of ride brings? How about the weather? Would you only ride when it's sunny and warm? How about a cold day with a chance of snow? Well, let's find out. It's time to saddle up.

Matthew 7:13-14 says, "Enter through the narrow gate; for the gate is wide and the way is broad that leads to destruction, and there are many who enter through it. For the gate is narrow and the way is constricted that leads to life, and there are few who find it."

Trail riding took on a whole new meaning when I decided to follow Jesus as my Lord and Savior. He became the one that I sought after. I made the decision to give Him the reins instead of going off on my own, choosing the path that I thought best. It has been a long, gradual process. I have made some poor choices even after deciding to follow

Him. I take off down my own trail from time to time. Every time I did that, I either ran into a dead end, having to turn around and come back, or it landed me in a world of trouble that made me wish I had never taken that turn. I learned through much trial and error that God is the only way. In John 14:6 Jesus says, "I am the way, and the truth, and the life; no one comes to the Father except through me." Not only does Christ tell us that He is the only way to the Father, but He also tells us that this is what we were created for. Ephesians 2:10 says, "For we are His workmanship, created in Christ Jesus for good works, which God prepared beforehand so that we would walk in them."

So, if He tells us that He is the only way to the Father and that is exactly what He created us to do, then isn't that the best plan for our lives? God *created* us to follow Him. He made us to be His companions, to be His children, to be His servants and He our Friend, our Father, our Master.

If you think you are going along just fine on your own and really don't understand why you should follow Jesus, read the Scripture in Matthew again, that part about the wide road leading to destruction. If your life has been fairly simple, not too many bumps and bruises so far, it could be possible that there's no reason for Satan to come after you because you are already his. You are on your way to destruction, and you don't even realize it.

Or maybe you have faced some hellacious obstacles, waterfalls and ditches, and there seems to be no way around or over. Maybe life has become so unbearable that you can't find peace in any situation or in any path you take. If this is you, then stop! Access the path and inspect the situation. Is it profitable to keep going down a path that just continues to lead to hard times with no peace? Maybe you have held the reins too long, and maybe it's time to give them to Him—Jesus Christ. Let Him "pony you," directing you along for a while. In the horse world, "ponying" is when you ride a well-trained horse and lead one who isn't so that the untrained horse learns by following the trained one. He knows the plan, and He knows the path even if you don't. Jeremiah 29:11 says, "'For I know the plans I have for you,' declares the Lord, 'plans for prosperity and not for disaster, to give you future and a hope.'"

How do I know which way to go? What should I do? Who do I turn to? Jeremiah 42:3 says, "[Pray] that the Lord will tell us the way in which we should walk, and the thing that we should do." The answer? Pray! Turn to God! Acts 3:19 says,"Therefore repent and return, so that your sins may be wiped away, in order that times of refreshing may come from the presence of the Lord."

Have you ever been on a long ride, hike, drive, or got turned around, or it just took a lot longer than you planned to get back home? Maybe you forgot to pack water and by the time you made it back you thought you would die from thirst. I know I have. When I have gone my own way before, not the way that God would have me go, I have been in situations where no matter how hard I tried, I found no comfort, no peace and no refreshment of any kind. Those have been some hard times. Those are the times that when I think back and remember them, it reminds me to turn to God before I just duck down any old path that shows up along the way. Some paths may look easier or you may be tricked into thinking they are a shortcut, but don't listen to the lies of the devil. Those trails end up causing more pain, more time or more trouble than you could possibly imagine. Pray and ask for forgiveness when you do make a wrong turn, read your Bible, and listen to Him for the direction that He would have you go. Then you will receive the living water from the well that never runs dry.

Just as preparing for trail rides is incredibly important, so is preparing for anything on this amazing ride called life. The things I need in my saddle bags that help me most are these: God's word, a personal relationship with Him, prayer, and other believers.

All Scripture is inspired by God and beneficial for teaching, for rebuke, for correction, for training in righteousness.
(2 Timothy 3:16)

The Bible is our trail map. The Bible is what we should go to everyday to help us stay on the path. We should study it and memorize it so that if we forget to carry it with us, we will have it in our hearts and minds.

Your word is a lamp for my feet, a light on my path.
(Psalm 119:105)

Those moonlit rides, those times when the light is dim, or maybe when the clouds form and you get no light at all, read His word. Those times when things get so dark that the trail disappears and you just can't see which way to go, the Bible is not only the map it is also the light! Talk about an amazing tool to pack along.

SINGING IN THE DARK

Wait for the LORD; be strong and take heart and wait for the Lord.
(Psalm 27:14)

When life is overwhelming and you panic, you get lost. Pull up and take a minute. Learn to wait on the Lord. He loves you and He will provide for your every need.

Do not fear, for I am with you; Do not be afraid, for I am your God. I will strengthen you, I will also help you, I will also uphold you with my righteous right hand.
(Isaiah 41:10)

Do not be anxious about anything, but in everything by prayer and pleading with thanksgiving let your requests be made known to God.
(Philippians 4:6-7)

Once there was a group of us riding in the mountains. We were up pretty high in altitude when a storm blew in. Thunder was rolling and lightning flashed. There was no place to go for shelter and no quick way to get down off that mountain. A barbed wire fence was off to the right side of the trail about twenty feet away. Lightning struck somewhere up ahead of us and the electricity ran down that wire, hissing and popping. I had never witnessed anything like that before, or anything like it since. Needless to say, we were frightened! The horses spooked, jumping and bolting. Praise God, no one was thrown or injured. Fear is of the devil. Fear paralyzes us and causes us to bolt. Prayer was most definitely our go to that day!

There have definitely been some "pucker moments" along the trails of my life. We are not promised to have easy trails, that's for certain. I still to this day struggle with trusting Him with all things in all ways during all situations, but I am getting better. Having a relationship with Him, praying and spending time in His word develops that relationship into one of trust and security. When you get to a point in your faith where no matter what happens on the ride, you know that paradise is waiting at the end, then you have attained hope. When you know that His Word is true, then you have a hope that no disaster on any trail can take away, no matter how long or how hard. That, my friends, is the hope of the Lord.

Having other believers to ride with you is a priceless commodity that God has so blessed me with. When you are likeminded with the people you share the trail with, the experience is so much better. They are there to encourage and help when things get tough, and you can help them as well.

Proverbs 12:26 says that "the righteous person is a guide to his neighbor, but the way of the wicked leads them astray."

I certainly don't need any help being led astray. I can do a pretty good job of that all by myself. Thank God, His mercies are new each day and He is quick to forgive a repentant heart.

1 Corinthians 15:33 says, "Do not be misled: 'Bad company corrupts good morals."

2 Corinthians 6:14 says, "Do not be mismatched with unbelievers; for what do righteousness and lawlessness share together, or what does light have in common with darkness?"

God's word specifically tells us what kind of people we should choose as our friends and what happens if we make the wrong choice.

John 15:12-15 says, "This is My commandment, that you love one another, just as I have loved you. Greater love has no one than this, that a person will lay down his life for his friends. You are My friends if you do what I command you. No longer do I call you slaves, for the slave does not know what his master is doing; but I have called you friends, because all things that I have heard from My Father I have made known to you."

Colossians 3:12-14 says, "So, as those who have been chosen of God, holy and beloved, put on a heart of compassion, kindness, humility, gentleness, and patience; bearing with one another, and forgiving each other, whoever has a complaint against anyone; just as the Lord forgave you, so must you do also"

Those are the people I want on the trail with me. Ones that will help in times of trouble, those who will point me in the right direction if I go the wrong way, or those who will come down that trail and bring me back if I get lost. They won't give up on me, they love me and they truly trust in God. These are the ones that are a part of the body of Christ. When I am with them, and we are riding along together, praising God, in communion with Him, that is the closest I have ever felt to Heaven.

So, have you figured out yet which trail you would take? How should you prepare for the ride?

It won't be much longer and spring will be here. Prime

trail riding time! I am excited. I am looking forward to spending time in the saddle, in God's creation, with my horse and my friends and Him. Just remember, "Whatever you do, do your work heartily, as for the Lord and not for people, knowing that it is from the Lord that you will receive the reward of the inheritance. It is the Lord Christ whom you serve" (Colossians 3:23-34).

Yes, even trail riding can and should be done unto the Lord, because that's what you were created for. Trust Him, pray always, seek out other believers and ride! What better way to praise our God than from on the back of a horse. Choose the right path and encourage others to follow Him as you go the only way.

Happy trails!

God, I praise you for the abundant trails you have created in this wonderful place and for the animals you have blessed me with to provide pleasure and to teach me about You. I am a poor steward of these gifts you have given me. Lead me and guide me in the way that you would have me go. Thank you for the Word you have given as our trail map. Amen.

Stuck

SINGING IN THE DARK

SINGING IN THE DARK

5/28/19

Have you ever been stuck? In a ditch, maybe? In a relationship? In a job? Emotionally? Have you ever been depressed, anxious, fearful, angry, resentful or bitter? Have you ever been stuck in a spiritual rut? Have you sinned and now you're stuck? Do you feel like you aren't growing in your faith or that God is distant and unreachable?

I have.

Yesterday was Memorial Day. Two friends of mine and I made plans to get up early, beat the heat, and go for a much-needed trail ride. We decided to go to a location that we haven't ridden in probably close to a year, so we knew that there was a good possibility we could be trailblazing or dodging obstacles.

Before my friends got to my house, I considered which horse I was going to ride. I could ride my recently-purchased horse, a nice mare named Willow, who is an easy going, relaxed trail horse. Or I could ride Little Bit. He is on the chopping block, meaning I am seriously considering selling him. I decided to ride him for two reasons: first, to make sure he is sound because about a month ago he injured himself and was unable to walk without limping. Second, I just wanted to have one last ride. Tacking him up was a little bittersweet.

One of my friends showed up to saddle her horse, which is boarded at my house. Shortly after, my other friend came riding up on her horse that she keeps just down the road. She and her horse were the only reasons that I was hesitant about riding Little Bit, since he gets anxious around unfamiliar horses, but I chose him anyway.

We started out my driveway, heading for the trails. Little Bit lived up to his name, moving slowly. He always takes a little bit. I had to steadily push him to keep up with the others. At that point he didn't seem to mind the strange mare up ahead of us. When we reached a trail head, we noticed that things were different. There was a huge house under construction where the trail used to be. No one was at the house, so instead of going around, we rode up the drive and right through the property to find the trail on the other side. Easy. We continued along the trail and found that someone had done a little clearing.

Several large fallen trees had been sawed and pulled out of the way. We reached the end of a trail where the path opens up to the road, and found a cable across the end of the trail that we would have to go around to get to the road. The trees and brush were thick on both sides. One friend went to one side to see if we could get through and I went to the other side. Neither side looked passable. I then went to the side my friend went on to have a look for myself. It wasn't so thick on that side but there was a small brush pile on the ground that we would have to go through to get out. It appeared that we were stuck.

This is where Little Bit showed his strengths, his training, and his trust in me. With the two friends following behind, Little Bit moved forward toward the brush with his head lowered to see where he needed to put his feet. He never hesitated–actually, I made him step back a bit so that I could assess the situation and make sure he wasn't going to hurt himself or me. Then when I gave him his head, he very carefully stepped through the brush, placing his hooves in precise spots to prevent getting tripped up or trapped.

The two behind me didn't have it so easy. The mare first balked, refusing, thinking she was stuck. Then she bolted through the brush, tripping, stumbling and nearly falling. The gelding behind her did the same, banging his legs on limbs and plunging through, not thinking of the consequences, just wanting to get to the other side. Oh, how I appreciated my horse at that moment.

I thought about our lives, how we sometimes get stuck, and how we handle our "stuck" situations. Do we take the time to assess the situation and find out what caused us to get stuck? Do we plunge ahead and do all that we can to just get through? Or, do we turn to Scripture, God's Word, our guide, our trail map. Isaiah 1:19 says, "If you are willing and obedient, you will eat the best of the land." This is the word of the Lord to the nation of Israel and it absolutely applies to us today. Romans 10:9 says, "If you confess with your mouth Jesus as Lord and believe in your heart that God raised Him from the dead, you will be saved." The promise is salvation. The *if*, or condition, is that you first confess and believe. Notice that both of these Scriptures have that two-letter word, *if*.

My horse didn't get that good on trails by himself. I started working with him long before riding him. When he was a foal, I would wrap ropes around his legs so that he would feel stuck. When he would relax, I would untangle him. He learned to trust me. Once I did start riding him, I would intentionally get him in a mess, then have him stop and stand in it, teaching him patience and that it was safer to be still until I could get him out of that mess. He soon realized that I was looking after him and would take care of him when he got himself in trouble.

I believe this is how God is with us when we get stuck. If I am willing and obedient, He will bless me and take care of me. If I confess with my mouth and believe, He saves me. If I submit to His will for my life just like my horse submits to me, I have salvation.

James 1:4 says, "And let endurance have its perfect result, so that you may be perfect and complete, lacking in nothing." With faith, we get started, and with patience, we finish the race–or in this case, the trail ride. When we first started out on this ride, we weren't sure what the trails were going to be like or what obstacles could possibly be in our way, but we went anyway, with faith. Once we got to the obstacle, it took patience to get safely to the other side. From that point on, it was wide roads, clear and safe. Spiritual patience is that force in our reborn spirit, based on our faith in the Word of God that will not quit.

I have gotten "stuck recently" Every time, I was in that situation because of something that I did. It wasn't because God had turned His back on me and left me alone to figure out my own messes, but rather because I sinned against Him.

I had been in a place of rebuke, correction, and chastisement for days. I have discovered that if I am in a true, obedient relationship with my Father, when I sin against Him, conviction is immediate and painful. I feel stuck in a place of regret and shame. Stuck in a place that I cannot move forward from. Jesus' death on the cross forgave us our sins, past, present, and future. His work, not mine. I cannot try to justify my sin, and I cannot try to blame others for my sin. When I cry out and God still seems distant, I read Scripture, pray, and beg for forgiveness. I will think twice before committing that sin again. I want to follow His will.

Like my relationship with my horse, I have figured out that just as I take care of Little Bit, God is taking care of me. Just like when Little Bit messes up, I chastise him and make him see his mistake, my heavenly Father does the same for me. My will is what gets me stuck, just like those other horses in the thicket. They were not being obedient to their masters; their will is what got them in trouble.

In the Lord's Prayer, Jesus gave us an example of how we should pray. He said, "Your kingdom come, *Your will* be done" (Matthew 6:10, emphasis added).

Psalm 119:10 says, "With all my heart I have sought You; Do *not let me wander* from Your commandments". Verse

37 says, "Turn my eyes away from looking at what is worthless, and revive me in Your ways".

Psalm 51:10 says, "Create in me a clean heart, God, and *renew a steadfast spirit* within me".

I began praying out loud for God to forgive me. I sang His praises and sought Him in every way I could. I know that these moments bring growth and a renewed relationship with Him. These times have led to a deeper, more intimate relationship. He loves me and He gives me every opportunity to get "unstuck."

Ephesians 5:15-17 says, "So then, be careful how you walk, not as unwise people but as wise, making the most of your time, because the days are evil. Therefore do not be foolish, but understand what the will of the Lord is." We can understand His will by having a relationship with Him, by prayer and His Word, and fellowship with His people.

1 Corinthians 10:13 says, "No temptation has overtaken you except something common to mankind; and God is faithful, so he will not allow you to be tempted beyond what you are able, but with the temptation will provide the way of escape also, so that you will be able to endure it."

After we came out onto the wide, clear road, with no obstacles and nothing for him to focus on, Little Bit lost his mind. He began acting like a fool. Suddenly, he felt that the mare became a threat to him when she ended up between himself and his pasture mate, nearly tossing me several times. In some situations, he can be an obedient and wonderful horse to ride, but in others he is not. He becomes anxious and unreliable, even dangerous.

Wow, am I like that for my Father? Can I lose my focus, get anxious, become unreliable and sometimes even dangerous to my testimony? Absolutely! Unlike my Master, I am inconsistent with my horse. I don't spend the time with Little Bit that I should, yet I still expect great behavior all the time. I have caused my horse to get stuck. Yes, I am going to sell Little Bit. He needs an owner that will correct and praise, rebuke and love him consistently. I pray that he will become the submissive creature of service that God made him to be. I pray that I can become the submissive daughter of service that He has called me to be. I pray that I can surrender all to Him so that I can become exactly what He wants me to be.

Oh God, what an amazing Master you are. Lord, You know I tend to get myself stuck from time to time. Please forgive me. Help me to be more obedient to Your will and Your way in my life. Thank You for the Holy Spirit that leads, guides, and walks with me every step I take. Amen.

SINGING IN THE DARK

Dirt Track Races

SINGING IN THE DARK

SINGING IN THE DARK

7/30/19

Last weekend, at the age of forty-nine years old, I experienced my very first dirt track race. What an experience! I've been to lawn mower races, tractor pulls, demolition derbies, but never a dirt track race. Jamey, on the other hand, is quite familiar with dirt track racing, since he used to race when he was younger. As we prepared to go, he packed a cooler and chairs. I packed snacks and Tylenol. He told me to put a couple pairs of safety glasses in my bag. I wanted to ask why, but refrained. Wearing jeans, flip flops, and a blue-and-white striped top, I now wonder why my husband didn't tell me that I shouldn't wear anything white.

We headed to Carolina Speedway, about an hour away from our home. We arrived a little early to get good seats. Sitting in the center of the stadium, I noticed that the top section was already full. As the practice laps started, Jamey told me about the different classes of cars, some smaller and slower, some larger and faster.

Soon, the races got underway, the smaller cars going first. The track was wet down and packed prior to any cars coming onto the track. During the first few races, no dust came up off of the track. I thought, *Why in the world do we need safety glasses?* A few races later, however, a little dust began to come up. As the night progressed and the cars got bigger and faster, the dust began to spread up into the stands, barely noticeable.

Finally, it was time for the late model class. I know *nothing* about race cars. Nothing at all. As the cars came onto the track, Jamey asked me to give him a pair of safety glasses and told me I may want to put a pair on as well. Then it was on! When the green flag was waved, the cars blew past us, spraying a cloud of red clay dust in every direction, including up.

Those cars were only on two tires going around the corners crazy fast, and it was a forty lap race! Caution flags flew from all the bumps and wrecks and breakdowns, causing a lot of slowing down and speeding up. I am so grateful that my husband looked out for me by bringing two pairs of safety glasses; they were definitely needed.

About halfway through the race, I noticed a light layer of dust all over Jamey and the other people sitting around us. I looked down at my jeans and my top to see that they were now a new color of light orange, no longer blue and white. By the end of the race, there wasn't a single part of anyone there that wasn't covered in red clay dust. But oh, how exciting that race was!

A couple days later, I was still thinking about the race–my very first dirt track race. Then, as though God were whispering in my ear, the lesson came to me. Like the first dust I felt gently settling on my skin, seemingly harmless, sin creeps into our lives.

Proverbs 4:23 says, "Watch over your heart with all diligence, for from it flow the springs of life."

Psalm 139:23-24 says, "Search me, God, and know my heart; put me to the test and know my anxious thoughts; And see if there is any hurtful way in me, And lead me in the everlasting way."

As I was sitting in the stands, everything seemed so good, just a little dust stirring up. But as things got faster and more exciting, the dust flew harder and eventually covered everyone and everything there. Even the cars parked on the backside of that huge stadium had the same coating of orange dust.

This is what happens when we choose to be around bad influences, or to be in situations that at first seem good. If we choose the wrong friends or put our faith in the wrong people, we may enter a situation where a little harmless dust stirs until, before we realize it, we're caught up in the excitement and dust starts flying. By the time it's over, we may be nearly unrecognizable.

The white stripes on my top were no longer white. When we got home late that night, we had to take showers before bed because we were filthy. There would be no "just dusting off." The dust was caked on. We even had to use Q-tips to get the mud out of our ears. We also used a lot of tissues to get all the mud boogers out!

Being in the wrong place with the wrong people can quickly cause us harm. Whether it has to do with sex, alcohol, drugs, or breaking the law, peer pressure is the excuse for all kinds of illegal and immoral behavior. Anybody who has ever developed godly character has had to fight against peer pressure, including Noah and his family, Abraham and his family, Moses in Egypt, and Daniel and his friends in Babylon. Resisting peer pressure means not just saying a determined "no" to people, but also a dedicated "yes" to the Lord.

Scripture instructs us to be careful in choosing the right friends:

> *But actually, I wrote to you not to associate with any so-called brother if he is a sexually immoral person, or a greedy person, or an idolater, or is verbally abusive, or habitually drunk, or a swindler–not even to eat with such a person.*
> (1 Corinthians 5:11)

> *Blessed is the person who does not walk in the counsel of the wicked, Nor stand in the path of sinners, Nor sit in the seat of scoffers! But his delight is in the Law of the Lord, And on His Law he meditates day and night. He will be like a tree planted by streams of water, Which yields its fruit in its season, And its leaf does not wither; And in whatever he does, he prospers. The wicked are not so, But they are like chaff which the wind blows away.*
> (Psalm 1:1-4)

Not only did those fine particles of dust settle on our clothing, in our hair, on our skin; but if it was in our ears and nostrils, then we also breathed it into our lungs. We internalized the dust. The same goes with sin. It enters our hearts. We may have layers on the outside that become visible to those around us over time, but more dangerous than that is what has changed on the inside.

> *That which comes out of the person, that is what defiles the person. For from within, out of the hearts of people, come the evil thoughts, acts of sexual immorality, thefts, murders, acts of adultery, deeds of greed, wickedness, deceit, indecent behavior, envy, slander, pride, and foolishness. All these evil things come from within and defile the person.*
> (Mark 7:20-23)

> *But the Lord said to Samuel, "Do not look at his appearance or at the height of his stature, because I have rejected him; for God does not see as man sees, since man looks at the outward appearance, but the Lord looks at the heart."*
> (1 Samuel 16:7)

No matter what we look like on the outside, whether the dust is visible to all, or if we've showered and washed our blue-and-white striped top so the stripes are white again, God sees what's within. And what's in our heart, comes out.

As Christians, we cannot allow that to happen. We must be careful, read God's word, trust Him, and pray for true godly friends to spend our lives with.

How do we cleanse ourselves? By the blood of Jesus! 1 John 1:7-9 says, "But if we walk in the light, as He Himself is in the light, we have fellowship with one another, and the blood of Jesus his Son cleanses us from all sin. If we say that we have no sin, we are deceiving ourselves and the truth is not in us. If we confess our sins, he is faithful and righteous, so that He will forgive us our sins and cleanse us from all unrighteousness."

After the blood of Jesus washes us white as snow, we have to work at keeping ourselves clean.

Colossians 3:12 says, "So, as those who have been chosen of God, holy and beloved, put on a heart of compassion, kindness, humility, gentleness, and patience."

When we pray for discernment and knowledge in choosing our friends and then ask God to send them our way, amazing things happen. Ecclesiastes 4:9-10 says, "Two are better than one because they have a good return for their labor; for If either of them falls, the one will lift up his companion. But woe to the one who falls when there is not another to lift him up!"

I remember when I chose ungodly friends and put myself in some 'dusty' situations. If anything happened that meant trouble of any kind, those 'friends' scattered–nowhere to be found! They certainly weren't hanging around to help me up if I fell.

Proverbs 11:14 (KJV) says, "Where no counsel is, the people fall: But in the multitude of counselors there is safety." When we are surrounded by people of godly character, our chances of falling are lower, but even when we do fall, godly friends will be there to help us; to pick us up.

That night at the track, I was internalizing that dust. I'd been struggling with summer cold symptoms–lots of coughing and congestion. I'd put off going to the doctor, and about four days later, I began having a hard time breathing, so I made an appointment. The doctor told me had I waited another day or so, I'd have been admitted to the hospital with pneumonia. My lungs were already compromised by the virus, and I'm sure the dust I inhaled didn't help matters at all. We are already compromised since we live in the world where Satan has dominion. We must choose not to inhale the dust.

We often think of the 'wrong crowd' as drug addicts or immoral people, the ones whose coating of dust is obvious, but that's not always the case. 1 John 4:1 (NASB) says, "Beloved do not believe every spirit, but test the spirits to see whether they are from God, because many false prophets have gone out into the world." The 'wrong crowd' may be members of our families, childhood friends, or even those sitting beside us in Bible study. They are often people we've known and loved a long time, and it may be incredibly difficult to separate from them. However, because of their attitude and their choices in life, they can play a huge part in the reason why we find it hard to receive what God would have for us in our own lives.

Here's what Scripture tells us to do when we are struggling with the world's dust:

> *Do not love the world nor the things in the world. If anyone loves the world, the love of the Father is not in him. For all that is in the world, the lust of the flesh and the lust of the eyes and the boastful pride of life, is not from the Father, but is from the world. The world is passing away*

SINGING IN THE DARK

and also its lusts; but the one who does the will of God continues to live forever.
(1 John 2:15-17)

But you did not learn Christ in this way, if Indeed you have heard Him and have been taught in Him, just as truth is in Jesus, that, in reference to your former way of life, you are to rid yourselves of the old self, which is being corrupted in accordance with the lusts of deceit, and that you are to be renewed in the spirit of your mind, and to put on the new self, which in the likeness of God has been created in righteousness and holiness of the truth.
(Ephesians 4:20-24)

Do not be mismatched with unbelievers; for what do righteousness and lawlessness share together, or what does light have in common with darkness?
(2 Corinthians 6:14)

This is not to say that we shouldn't have a job working with unbelievers, or we shouldn't minister to or love or counsel the ungodly. Not at all! We just have to be cautious of who we choose to "yoke" ourselves since they will influence us. Proverbs 27:17 says, "As iron sharpens iron, so one person sharpens another." When you have godly friends, the Father can use them to help keep you on the course to His desired destination for your life. Likewise, if you're a godly friend you can be used by Him to do the same for others. Having the right friends is great. We all need people to share our experiences with–even the dusty ones!

I read this somewhere and found it to be very true: Everyone needs a Jonathan, someone on equal par with us, someone to share life experiences with, someone we can sharpen and depend on to help keep us sharp.

Dear Father, I praise You, God for forming man of the dust of the ground and breathing into his nostrils the breath of life. I praise You for creating me in Your image. Lord, you know that this flesh is weak. Forgive us when we allow that very dust that You used to create us to cause us to stumble. Lord, I ask You today to provide us with Your Word, to cleanse our hearts and to give us others to learn from, to lean on and to teach Your ways. Protect us from all evil. Thank You Lord for the many blessings You give us each day. Thank You for giving us the ability to know who we should be yoked with. Thank You for Your Word and the Holy Spirit that helps us. Thank You for the friend we have in Jesus! It's in His holy name I pray. Amen.

SINGING IN THE DARK

Dogs and Skunks

SINGING IN THE DARK

SINGING IN THE DARK

9/3/19

No one is to say when he is tempted, "I am being tempted by God"; for God cannot be tempted by evil, and He Himself does not tempt anyone. But each one is tempted when he is carried away and enticed by his own lust. Then when lust has conceived, it gives birth to sin; and sin, when it has run its course, brings forth death. Do not be deceived, my beloved brothers and sisters. Every good thing given and every perfect gift is from above, coming down from the Father of lights, with whom there is no variation or shifting shadow. In the exercise of His will He gave us birth by the word of truth, so that we would be a kind of first fruits among His creatures.
(James 1:13-18)

Now when He arrived at the place, He said to them, "Pray that you do not come into temptation."
(Luke 22:40)

In the Luke passage, Jesus tells His disciples to pray as He pleads with the Father. When He returns, He finds them sleeping and tells them again to rise and pray lest they enter into temptation.

SINGING IN THE DARK

In Matthew 6:13, Jesus gives us an example of how we should pray: "And do not lead us into temptation but deliver us from evil."

One morning around 5:00, I woke up and smelled skunk while in my bed with doors and windows closed, air conditioning on. I remembered letting my little dog, Chex, out earlier, so I knew immediately what had happened. Chex had been sprayed. Again. This was the fifth time that dog has been sprayed in the two years that he has lived with us. Why, oh why, does Chex keep on getting sprayed? Why hasn't he figured out yet that those cute, furry little things make him miserable *and* stinky if he messes with them?

After this most recent incident, I did a little research. Skunks are described as "a gentle species," easy-going, non-aggressive in nature, and unintentionally bothersome. They usually give ample warning by hissing, growling, stamping their feet and bushing up their tail, prior to spraying. They are solitary, living and foraging alone. They are most active at night, more so at early dawn or dusk. They have a ten-foot spray range. The spray is made up of oils and thiols (sulfuric chemicals) that are very difficult to remove. They also carry rabies.

As I did the research, I began thinking of how some of those qualities relate to sin in our lives. Think about one particular sin that is just so incredibly hard to resist. Maybe it's non-aggressive, or unintentionally bothersome; maybe it has 'warning signs,' or maybe it's attractive and pretty. If that's not enough and you're bitten, you could die.

So, why doesn't my dog get it? Does that skunk so closely resemble a cat that it fools Chex into thinking he can play with it? Or is Chex's drive to hunt so strong that he can't resist getting defensive and protective of his territory? Or is he just dumb and forgetful? Isn't sin to us like that skunk to Chex? Do we ask ourselves why we repeat that same sin over and over? Is it attractive? Is it tricky? Do we have an overwhelming desire? Are we forgetful? Do we feel plain dumb sometimes when we fall into temptation yet again? Whatever sin it is, there is hope.

Romans 5:8 says, "But God demonstrates His own love toward us, in that while we were still sinners, Christ died for us."

But it doesn't end there! 1 Corinthians 15:3-4 says, "For I handed down to you as of first importance what I also received, that Christ died for our sins according to the Scriptures, and that He was buried, and that He was raised on the third day according to the Scriptures." Praise God!

But, what can we do to try and prevent that dog from getting sprayed again?

Going back to the research, I found that skunks are attracted to pet food left outside. That's easy enough, just don't leave dog food outside. Avoid letting inside dogs out during the night, unless they are on a leash. Skunks like to build their dens under open porches or elevated sheds and buildings, wood piles and such. Maybe we need to eliminate access to those areas. Also, making noise before turning a dog out can frighten the skunk away. Remember, skunks are nocturnal, they don't like bright light. We can light things up!

In relation to our sin, if we have accepted Jesus as our Lord and Savior, then His light is in us! We must avoid darkness and physical temptations. Surround ourselves with godly people who can keep us 'on a leash' or hold us accountable. And they can make noise by *praying* for us!

James 4:7 says, "Submit therefore to God. But resist the devil, and he will flee from you."

Stay out of the ten-foot spray range! Pray for God to help you curb the desire to sin. If you ask forgiveness for a repeated sin with no intention to stop, then your heart is not in the right place. God can and will help you with the struggle of repeated sin if you ask. He will forgive *every time* if you truly repent and seek forgiveness. Your intent is the key. God knows our hearts. Sin is a part of life and God knows that too.

The Bible says that "if we walk in the light, as He Himself is in the light, we have fellowship with one another, and the blood of Jesus His Son cleanses us from all sin. If we say that we have no sin, we are deceiving ourselves and the truth is not in us. If we confess our sins, He is faithful and righteous, so that He will forgive us our sins and cleanse us from all unrighteousness" (1 John 1:7-9).

That means *boundless* forgiveness *if* there is repentance.

> *The Lord is not slow about His promise, as some count slowness, but is patient toward you, not willing for any to perish, but for all to come to repentance.*
> (2 Peter 3:9)

> *Therefore, since we have a great high priest who has passed through the heavens, Jesus the Son of God, let's hold firmly to our confession. For we do not have a high priest who cannot sympathize with our weaknesses, but One who has been tempted in all things just as we are, yet without*

sin. Therefore let's approach the throne of grace with confidence, so that we may receive mercy and find grace for help at the time of our need.
(Hebrews 4:14-16)

These words should not allow us to keep sinning, but rather they should encourage us to keep repenting, to bring our sin to the Savior who bathes us in His blood!

Along with that, I thought of how to get rid of the stench of my little dog's poor choices. I usually do one of two things: a tomato juice bath or a mixture of hydrogen peroxide, baking soda, and Dawn dish detergent. Maybe Chex likes the horrible smell and would choose of his own accord to bask in it for however long it would take to wear off. However, I do know that he enjoys coming inside, so I make the choice for him to wash it off.

Jesus gives us His body and His "blood of the covenant" to remove the stench of our sin:

Now while they were eating, Jesus took some bread, and after a blessing, He broke it and gave it to His disciples, and said, "Take and eat, this is my body." And when He had taken a cup, given thanks, He gave it to them, saying, "Drink from it, all of you; for this is My blood of the covenant, which is being poured out for many for forgiveness of sins.
(Matthew 26:26-28)

Jesus offers Himself for us to take if we choose so that we may repent and be forgiven. There's no such thing as too much sin, only too little faith.

Be gracious to me, God, according to Your faithfulness;

According to the greatness of Your compassion, wipe out my wrongdoings. Wash me thoroughly from my guilt and cleanse me from my sin. For I know my wrongdoings, and my sin is constantly before me. Against You, You only, I have sinned and done what is evil in Your sight, so that You are justified when You speak and blameless when You judge. . . . Purify me with hyssop, and I will be clean; Cleanse me, and I will be whiter than snow. Let me hear joy and gladness, let the bones you have broken rejoice. Hide your face from my sins and wipe out all my guilty deeds. Create in me a clean heart, God, and renew a steadfast spirit within me. Do not cast me away from Your presence, and do not take Your Holy spirit from me. Restore to me the joy of Your salvation, and sustain me with a willing spirit. Then I will teach wrong-doers Your ways, and sinners will be converted to You.
(Psalm 51:1-5, 7-13)

Now that I know more about skunks, and what to do to help my little dog avoid them, or what to do if he happens to get too close again, I want to share that with others. Hopefully I can help someone else avoid the consequences of their own dog's temptation. Better yet, maybe I can help someone else turn to God in their sin and know the peace that comes with repentance and forgiveness!

Heavenly Father, You are Almighty God, the Creator of all things, even those stinky little creatures that cause me distress. I admit, Lord, that I all too often am tempted to sin and fail miserably. I ask You Lord, to please forgive me when I fail You. Help me learn from my sin and remember the stink that comes from it. Thank You Father for Your unending mercy! Thank you for loving a wretched sinner like me. Amen.

Family

SINGING IN THE DARK

10/14/19

What does "family" mean?

This is a difficult question to answer and is highly subjective. Since the word has entered our language the meaning has changed considerably. The earliest use of the term family meant a group of persons in the service of an individual. In a sense, that is now archaic. The word comes from the Latin *familia* which meant "household," a term that included both servants and relatives.

In the Meriam-Webster Dictionary I found several definitions:

1. The basic unit in society traditionally consisting of two parents rearing their children.
2. A group of individuals living under one roof and usually under one head; household.
3. A group of persons of common ancestry
4. A group of people united by certain convictions or a common affiliation; fellowship
5. A group of things related by common characteristics.

After reading Webster's definition, I looked up *family* in the Urban Dictionary, and ironically, I like its definition better: "A group of people, usually of the same blood (but do not have to be), who genuinely love, trust, care about, and look out for each other." Not to be mistaken with relatives sharing the same household who hate each other, a real family is a bond that cannot be broken by any means.

My 'traditional' family: my mom, dad, brother, husband, children, in-laws, aunts, uncles, cousins, nieces, and nephews are relatively close. We get together regularly and stay connected, for the most part. We are blessed that we all live within a short distance from one another so it is easy to all come together. There are members of my family that I feel connected to in a spiritual way which gives a whole new dimension to those relationships. Family is not easy, but I thank God for each one of my family members. Overall, I see other families and their struggles, and I realize that my family is truly blessed to not have a tremendous amount of drama or separation in any area. There is love in our family. God is the leader of our family and I know that is what holds us together. He is the glue.

In our church's Bible study, we have been studying the book of Genesis. We read:

> *The Lord said to Abram, 'Go from your country, and from your relatives and from your father's house, to the land which I will show you; And I will make you into a great nation, and I will bless you, and make your name great; and you shall be a blessing; and I will bless those who bless you and the one who curses you I will curse. And in you all the families of the earth will be blessed.*
> (Genesis 12:1-3)

As we read through those verses, I couldn't help but wonder if I could be as obedient as Abram if God told me to leave my family. It would not be easy. But then God told Abraham that through him all families would be blessed. That's your family, my family; *our* family! Abraham had no idea the magnitude of the words God spoke to him.

But there's *another* family. The family of God who promises, "And I will be a father to you, and you shall be sons and daughters to Me" (2 Corinthians 6:18).

Praise God! John 1:12-13 says:

But as many as received Him, to them He gave the right to become children of God, to those who believe in His name, who were born, not of blood, nor of the will of the flesh, nor of the will of a man but of God.

This is good stuff! Ephesians 2:19-22 says:

So then you are no longer strangers and foreigners, but you are fellow citizens with the saints, and are of God's household, having been built on the foundation of the apostles and prophets, Christ Jesus Himself being the cornerstone, in whom the whole building, being fitted together, is growing into a holy temple in the Lord, in whom you also are being built together into a dwelling of God in the Spirit.

The devil fears connection! He wants nothing more than to divide us. He despises the unity of family, whether traditional or spiritual.

Matthew 12:25-26 says:

And knowing their thoughts, Jesus said to them, "Every

kingdom divided against itself is laid waste; and no city or house divided against itself will stand. And if Satan is casting out Satan, he has become divided against himself; how then will his kingdom stand?"

Have you ever felt a connection with a complete stranger? You meet them for the first time and know immediately that spiritually you are brothers or sisters in Christ Jesus? The common bond is His blood. Hebrews 2:11 says that believers can claim Jesus as their brother:

For both He who sanctifies and those who are sanctified are all from one Father; for this reason He is not ashamed to call them brothers and sisters.

I've experienced it more than once, that feeling of knowing someone, connecting with them when you've never met before and have no human explanation for it. I believe that's how the Holy Spirit works. I believe just as John recognized Jesus from his mother's womb to Mary's womb, the Holy Spirit shows us those He dwells within. If you are blessed to have a relationship with those that you feel that connection with, then praise God for it! That is *family*. Along with the spiritual connection, comes the pain of sharing their burdens and struggles as well as their joys and victories in Jesus.

In 1 Corinthians 12, Paul talks about the body of Christ, the believers who make up that body, and its parts. That is this 'spiritual family' that I am talking about. Paul says, "And if one part of the body suffers, all the parts suffer with it; if a part is honored, all the parts rejoice with it. Now you are Christ's body, and individually parts of it" (12:26-27).

SINGING IN THE DARK

Last Monday, October 7, at Tri-County Cowboy Church, just as the service was starting, we began singing one of my favorite praise songs, "Father I Praise You," written by my brother, the incredibly talented Greg McDougal. Even before the singing started, I felt the Holy Spirit moving in an overwhelming way. Over a very short period of time, I had been made aware of some incredible struggles going on in multiple members of my spiritual family. It seemed like right at that moment, just before that song began, it all came flooding to my mind and heart.

The words, "Lord, forgive me, I don't even know how I ought to pray," made me realize that when so many difficulties come about at the same time, it's hard to even know what to ask, how to ask, or what to even say to God. I kept thinking about the tragic events that were affecting my brothers and sisters and the heartbreak that they were enduring. I couldn't speak, and I could barely think of getting through the next few songs. How God must grieve to see His children struggle. *But God!* He is the *Head* of the *household*. He is in control! He knows the plans He has for us, and our hope is in Him.

And if the Spirit of him who raised Jesus from the dead is living in you, he who raised Christ from the dead will also give life to your mortal bodies because of his Spirit who lives in you. Therefore, brothers and sisters, we have an obligation—but it is not to the flesh, to live according to it. For if you live according to the flesh, you will die; but if by the Spirit you put to death the misdeeds of the body, you will live. For those who are led by the Spirit of God are the children of God. The Spirit you received does not make you slaves, so that you live in fear again; rather, the Spirit you

SINGING IN THE DARK

received brought about your adoption to sonship. And by him we cry, "Abba, Father."
(Romans 8:11-15, NIV)

Praise God!

In our traditional families, our leaders, our head of the household will let us down and fail us miserably at times. Our heavenly Father, however, is the perfect Father. He gives us instruction and gives us the perfect example to follow. He tells us in His word how to treat others and how to be obedient to Him:

If someone says, "I love God," and yet he hates his brother or sister, he is a liar; for the one who does not love his brother and sister whom he has seen, cannot love God, whom he has not seen.
(1 John 4:20)

So then, while we have opportunity, let's do good to all people, and especially to those who are of the household of the faith.
(Galatians 6:10)

He also tells us that He will never leave us or forsake us. I have hope and peace and contentment in knowing who my Father is. I find joy in the members of my spiritual family that God has placed in my life, the ones with whom I am blessed to develop relationships *and* those that I may only meet for a brief period of time.

I praise You, O God, my loving and most precious Father. Forgive me, Lord, when I forget what a good Father I have!

SINGING IN THE DARK

Please Lord, bless my family, the one that I was born into here on this earth and the one You chose to put me in through Your adoption. Thank You Father, for Your sons and daughters, my brothers and sisters. Thank You for being the perfect example of what a father should be. Lord, please breathe new life into Your people. Raise up a mighty army from dry bones so that all nations come to know that Jesus Christ is Lord. Amen.

SINGING IN THE DARK

Yielding

SINGING IN THE DARK

SINGING IN THE DARK

1/19/20

Then I heard the voice of the Lord, saying: "Whom shall I send, And who will go for Us?" Then I said, "Here am I! Send me."
(Isaiah 6:8)

When I was a year old, my parents gave my brother, who is two years older than me, a beautiful palomino Shetland pony for his birthday. Little did they know how much that gift for my brother would change my life. I fell in love with that pony. My brother really didn't care for her much, so she became mine. That was the beginning of a life-long love of horses. We lived on a farm with beef cattle, pigs, and chickens, however, my parents knew nothing about horses or ponies. Everything that I know today, I learned on my own, through a lot of trial and error. Thankfully, Beauty, the Shetland pony, was gentle and well-trained. For the first four years, I had to depend on my dad or grandfather to saddle that pony for me or lift me onto her back and lead her around. I wasn't big enough to ride her by myself. But it wasn't long until I was mounting her unassisted and riding bareback all by myself!

As soon as I was old enough to read, I began educating

myself on horses. I wanted to know everything there was to know. My mom ordered a magazine, *Horse of Course*, so that I could learn as much as possible. I would read them over and over until the cover would fall off. And of course, I would use what I read on that poor pony. She was either the best trained or the most messed up pony in the state by the time I was thirteen and my parents finally gave her to another little girl.

Throughout my life, I have had the pleasure of working with many horses on many levels of training, but the horse I learned the most from was Little Bit, the colt born from my mare, Ruby. By the time Little Bit was born, I was in my thirties and felt ready to start raising a horse from the ground up. I began working with him, imprinting him, on the day he was born. I desensitized him to 'scary' objects, tied his legs up with ropes, tightened belts and ropes around his girth, under his tail, and around his head and neck. At only a month old, that horse wasn't afraid of anything being on him. I also taught him to yield to pressure. I could push anywhere on him, and he would move away from the pressure. He would yield.

The word *yield* means "to surrender or submit (oneself) to another," "to give way to or become succeeded by someone or something else," or "to give in to pressure."

I had developed a relationship with this colt to build trust. He knew that I wasn't going to hurt him and he knew that I was going to take care of him, so he was willing to submit to me when I asked. As he grew older and became able to begin carrying a saddle and rider, he was very easy to train. It was no trouble to start riding him. He never bucked or reared. I line drove him and put objects on his back and taught him to yield since he was born so that when we put a rider on his back, it was just another day, another thing, and he took it all in stride.

One day my brother-in-Christ asked if he and his wife could come ride. I put him on Little Bit. He did really well with him. Several weeks later, I was talking to my friend and told him that I was working on some dates for a trail ride where a group of us could pack our Bibles in our saddle bags and hit the trail, stopping along the way for devotions and prayer. He was definitely interested. When I told him that I would have him ride Little Bit, he said that he and Little Bit would have to work on avoiding trees on the trail. On the previous ride, his legs bumped into several trees, leaving his knees bruised. I instructed him to put pressure with his leg on Little Bits' side, and the horse would move away from the pressure. He thought that was pretty cool. There's a message in that!

God's children are to God as horses are to their masters. There are so many things you can relate to-when it comes to us and our heavenly Father to horses and trainers. But this concept of *yielding* is something I struggle with. My rebellious nature wants to do things its own way. There are horses like that too. Some are easygoing and willing to do what its trainer asks. I call them "pleasers." They long to please their master. Unfortunately, I am not that way. I am the one that, left alone to her own devices, will go the wrong way, just to see what it's like or to prove that I can do it. That attitude has led me to some pretty dark places in my life. Even after I found Jesus and began my walk with Him, I would–and still do–have moments of rebellious independence, unyielding resistance.

God's Word tells us over and over again to submit, to be obedient, to yield:

Submit therefore to God. But resist the devil, and he will flee from you.
(James 4:7)

Therefore humble yourselves under the mighty hand of God, so that He may exalt you at the proper time.
(1 Peter 5:6)

Remind them to be subject to rulers, to authorities, to be obedient, to be ready for every good deed.
(Titus 3:1)

These verses reveal that if we yield, the devil will flee from us and Christ will exalt us. Yielding will prepare us for every good work! These are just some of the rewards of being obedient and yielding to Him.

Even Jesus learned obedience from the things He suffered as indicated in Hebrews 5:5-10:

So too Christ did not glorify Himself in becoming a high priest, but it was He who said to Him, "You are My Son, today I have Fathered You"; just as He also says in another passage, "You are a Priest forever according to the order of Melchizedek." In the days of His humanity, He offered up both prayers and pleas with loud crying and tears to the One able to save Him from death, and He was heard because of His devout behavior. Although He was a Son, He learned obedience from the things which He suffered. And having been perfected, He became the source of eternal salvation for all those who obey Him, being designated by God as High Priest according to the order of Melchizedek.

In Luke 22:42 Jesus pleads with the Father:

"Father, if you are willing, remove this cup from Me; yet not My will, but Yours, be done."

In Matthew 11:29 Jesus speaks to the multitudes, saying, "Take my yoke upon you, and learn from me, for I am gentle and humble in heart, and you will find rest for your souls." This Scripture reminds me of my job driving a stagecoach at the Buffalo Ranch when I was a teenager. While learning how to drive teams of horses, I came to understand what it means to be yoked. In some teams I used, one horse would work much harder than the other one, throwing his shoulders into the collar and leaning forward, pushing all his weight and strength into the load. The other horse would be lazy, strolling along, letting its partner do all the work. This imbalance would aggravate me. I felt bad for the horse that was doing all the work. But this is exactly what Jesus is saying to us in this Scripture. Yoke yourself to me and come along, but I have done the work.

Jesus said, "Take my yoke." He doesn't force it on us, but He is telling us to do this. If we choose to yoke ourselves with Him, we become humble and find rest for our souls. If we choose to yoke ourselves to Him, we must yield, be obedient, be submissive. If we don't, we will get ourselves in trouble. Bad things will happen.

When we train horses, we want them to be soft and supple to our prompting. By "soft and supple," I mean we want them to respond immediately when given a command. We want them to yield quickly and quietly to pressure. When a horse is well into his training, I should not have to dig a spur into his side to get him to move away from my leg. I want to be able to barely squeeze and feel an immediate response. Ideally, ultimately, I would love my horse to almost read my mind and respond to the most subtle of cues. This takes a *lot* of time spent together. It takes dedication–the same kind of dedication God wants us to have for Him. We must spend time in His Word. We have to know the Master to know His will in our life. We have to focus on Him, listening for His voice.

The author of Hebrews says that Jesus, "having been perfected, . . . became the source of eternal salvation for all those who obey Him, being designated by God as High Priest according to the order of Melchizedek. Concerning him we have much to say, and it is difficult to explain, since you have become poor listeners" (Hebrews 5:9-11). Ouch! Poor listeners. His target audience was obviously not yielding to the Lord's will in their lives. They had become dull in hearing–dull to the cues and commands given them. They were disobedient.

The Bible is full of examples of what happens when God's people are disobedient or unyielding. The Bible is also full of examples of what happens when God's people yield to The Master.

I want to be that one who says, "Yes, Lord, here I am, send me!" Obedient and yielding to every cue, every command.

SINGING IN THE DARK

Father, I pray today that I, along with my brothers and sisters in Christ, will look to our Master. I pray that we will be focused on Him with all that we are and then be quick to yield. Quick to move, go, do whatever it is He asks of us. I praise God, the Master of my soul, for being such a loving, kind, and gentle Master. I ask that He forgive me when I am poor at hearing, slow to move, or rebellious, and backing away when I should be moving forward. I pray He forgives me when I don't trust Him and decide to do things my way. Help us, Lord, to recognize that when we take Your yoke and yield to You, our burdens are light. Help us understand Your will in our lives and help us to glorify You in all that we do. Thank You, Father, for Your Word, Your example, and Your love. In the Holy name of Jesus Christ, our Lord and Savior, Amen.

SINGING IN THE DARK

A Masterpiece

SINGING IN THE DARK

SINGING IN THE DARK

2/19/2020

For we are His workmanship, created in Christ Jesus for good works, which God prepared beforehand so that we would walk in them.
(Ephesians 2:10)

Some versions of the Bible use the word masterpiece instead of *workmanship*.

Me? A Masterpiece? Wow! It's hard for me to believe that I am God's masterpiece, but I cannot let those lies penetrate any deeper. That's not what my Creator thinks.

When I listen to the truth, which is His Word–not my thoughts–then I hear Him say things like, "Oh, Deena, you don't always get it right, but I love you so much. I want you to see what I see, My beautiful creation, My treasure, My workmanship, My masterpiece."

Poiema: (poy-ay-mah) Greek word for workmanship, masterful creativity.

This word is used only twice in Scripture, once in

Ephesians 2:10 as quoted previously, and once in Romans 1:20 which says,

For since the creation of the world His invisible attributes, that is, His eternal power and divine nature, have been clearly perceived, being understood by what has been made, so that they are without excuse.

In these passages, it takes five English words to translate poiema, referring to the material creation. The world is not the result of a chance evolutionary process, but rather the direct result of the creative work of the Eternal God.

Poiema is also the English word for "poem."

Synonyms for this word include: showpiece, blockbuster, success, gem, jewel, prize, treasure, and piece of the master. As a freelance visual artist, I have been blessed with a gift from God to see things differently than many people see them. I reproduce the images I see in drawings or paintings. I'm constantly looking for my next inspiration. Sometimes, ideas come from something I see; sometimes, inspiration comes from something I hear or read; and sometimes it comes from what someone tells me. I now know that all inspiration, in whatever form, comes from God. I have learned that I have to scribble my inspiration down or make a quick sketch, or I tend to forget.

Yet there are times when an image becomes so imprinted in my mind's eye that I never forget it.

I was driving from the school to the pharmacy in town. I reached a railroad crossing and had to wait for the train. Just beside the train tracks there was a partially shaded garden spot, with freshly tilled soil. An elderly gentleman farmer in overalls and a straw hat was pushing his hand plow through the soil, making a row for a vegetable of his choice. He had worked about halfway down the row when the locomotive came barreling down the tracks. It was a cargo train pulling many metal box cars. Those box cars are the perfect canvas for some of the most amazing graffiti artists, and for the inexperienced artists who are just trying their hand at something illegal and have no business holding a spray can for any reason. I love graffiti. And yes, I admit, I can be pretty judgmental when it comes to art. As the box cars thundered by, I realized the farmer never missed a step in his work. He continued on as though the rush of the train was a simple springtime breeze. What a clash of culture! As the box cars kept coming like an endless moving gallery, an art show rattling away, I only wished the train were moving slower so that I could appreciate each piece. Instead, I only got a quick glimpse of each one.

The little old man continued on his way, pushing his plow, not even completing a single row by the time the gallery reached its end. He never looked up from his work as all of those images passed by in his peripheral vision. Maybe this was such an ordinary event to him that he thought nothing of it. Maybe he was so intent on his job that he didn't get distracted by the noise. Maybe there was an urgency to plant the seed. Or, maybe the train was nothing more than a nuisance that he had to work to ignore. Whatever the case may be, I know that the farmer paid no attention to the imagination, creativity, and time spent on each of those wheeled metal boxes clattering to who-knows-what destination.

SINGING IN THE DARK

Oh, how I want to paint this picture! I want to capture all that the moment has to hold. One piece of work caught my attention above all the others and will take center stage in the still arrangement that I design. It was painted in beautiful shades of blue against the steel gray metal. The name tagged was the name above all names, Jesus, creatively shaped into a fish. Once I saw that image, I focused on it, not seeing any other piece until it was out of sight. It was so well done—the light blues highlighting, the very dark blues giving such dimension that it seemed like the letters would fly off the fast-moving box car at any time.

That scene makes me think of 2 Corinthians 5:17 which says, "Therefore, if anyone is in Christ, this person is a new creation." My life, as any other believer's life, is like that train. Each car represents a part of our lives until Jesus appears. After that, nothing else is the same. Now the new creation is what matters and that is Jesus.

As I pondered the *Jesus* image, I was struck by the irony of what I saw. An artist attempted to create a masterpiece on the side of a box car using the name of the Master Himself. The Master as the Son, Jesus. The One who created the artist is now being recognized by the artist. That's what I want to do. I want to give Him the glory and honor for all that I am and all that I have. As 1 Corinthians 10:31 instructs, "Whatever you do, do it all for the glory of God."

1 Peter 4:11 says:

Whoever speaks is to do so as one who is speaking actual words of God; whoever serves is to do so as one who is serving by the strength which God supplies; so that is all things God may be glorified through Jesus Christ, to whom belongs the glory and dominion forever and ever. Amen.

In Ephesians, Paul says that we are God's masterpiece, created anew in Christ Jesus—so, we can do the good things He planned for us long ago. He didn't create us to sit and look pretty, to be hung on a wall or painted on a box car for all to admire. He created us for His plan, for His glory, not ours! The farmer, planting his garden is God's masterpiece, hopefully doing work for His glory.

Throughout my life as an artist, I've created a lot of work. A lot of that work glorified me. I took the credit. I've done many pieces for many people. Like those cargo cars, it was meaningless work because I hadn't seen Jesus yet. I hadn't accepted Him. Then that one box car came along with the name and changed it all. When Jesus came into my life, it changed everything, even my art and how I approached it. I began to think of how I could glorify Him instead of myself.

It's definitely been a process. I have to humble myself regularly, asking God to show me what I can do to glorify Him in every place, in every situation, in my job–even in my leisure time, riding a horse, spending time with my husband, my children, and my friends. I am amazed at how He has revealed Himself to me. He can reveal Himself as I sit at a railroad crossing, waiting patiently to go on with my busy life.

That moment at the tracks has revealed several lessons to me. First, "to be still and know that I am God" (Psalm 46:10), which was quite obvious. The second lesson revealed to me wasn't immediately clear. We, as His masterpiece, can glorify Him in anything we do, whether it be the plowing of a garden or in the art produced by someone commissioning them to create specific pieces for them. I am weak and small, but I am a masterpiece in His eyes. My mere human imagination is nothing. When God imagines something, it becomes real, living, and multidimensional. Since Jesus, my life–my art—has taken on a new dimension.

Yes, now that I've jumped on that Jesus train, I am a masterpiece! God has a plan for us. Artists and farmers. I believe that God's plan for me at this time is to retire from the school system in a few months to focus my art, my leisure, and my riding lessons on Him. All the ideas that come to my mind are of God. He is opening doors that I never thought possible. I am excited about the future and the possibilities it holds because I have Jesus leading the way, clattering down the track and tilling the soil. I pray that as I tell others that my talent is from God, that my parents say I was drawing as soon as I was able to hold a pencil in my tiny fingers, that seeds will be sown, that my work will be done as unto the Lord. I pray that someone will see something I have done and know that they are the masterpiece of the One and only Creator of all things!

I am the imperfect clay that the Lord is forever recreating into something new and perfect as Isaiah prays:

But now, Lord, You are our Father; we are the clay, and You our potter; And all of us are the work of Your hand.
(Isaiah 64:8)

I am the silver, watched over by the silversmith, in the fire, being refined as Malachi describes:

And He will sit as a smelter and a purifier of silver, and He will purify the sons of Levi and refine them like gold and silver, so that they may present to the Lord offerings in righteousness.
(Malachi 3:3)

We are His workmanship, His *masterpiece*.

Oh God, my Creator, Master of my soul, You alone know me. You made me who I am. You are the master artist, the potter, the jeweler, the painter of our lives. You create our sunrises, our sunsets, our landscapes, and our portraits. Lord, forgive me for the many failed opportunities throughout my life. Forgive me for my plagiarism, for taking credit for Your work.

Jesus prayed, "I glorified You on the earth by accomplishing the work You have given me to do" (John 17:4). God, I hope to be able to pray that prayer too. I pray, God, that You will bless all that I do, and that it will honor You, Lord. I ask that all who see art from me, will acknowledge that beauty as a gift from You! Keep me humble. Help me Father, to glorify You in all that I do. Thank You Lord for the gifts that You give Your children. Thank You for making us Your masterpiece. Thank You for Jesus and for saving me and making me a new creation through Him. Thank you for loving me that much! Amen.

SINGING IN THE DARK

SINGING IN THE DARK

On My Knees

SINGING IN THE DARK

SINGING IN THE DARK

4/23/20

This year will be in the history books. The corona virus has gotten some serious attention worldwide. Almost everything has been shut down–including churches, schools, and businesses–to prevent the spread of this deadly, infectious disease. I have much compassion for those who have been sick and for those who have lost loved ones (550 deaths in North Carolina alone, so far) or have suffered from the loss of their job. I feel for those who are suffering and will continue to suffer whether physically, mentally, financially, or spiritually. However, from the beginning of this astronomical threat to society, I have been excited to see what God will do!

Now, here we are, several months into quarantine, and I have seen many ways that He is working in the lives of so many. People are forced to slow down, spend time with loved ones, and learn to enjoy quiet time. People are turning to God for answers to their many questions. They are forced to lean on Him because the distractions and everything else they have depended on are now gone. Of course, there is still plenty of evil in this world, as there always will be on this side of eternity, but there is an awful lot of love being shown: God's work being done.

I think the one thing I truly miss is the time of fellowship with brothers and sisters, our Bible studies, and worship services since it has been mandated that we cannot meet. A few of us have continued to gather, but for the safety of all, we have followed the rules as God's Word says we should. I miss singing, praising and worshiping our Lord together as a body. I miss laughing and joking, hugging and crying together. I miss sharing meals and having tea or coffee over a good lesson. I miss openly sharing our concerns with one another and praying together, hand in hand. I miss praising God for answered prayers and celebrating victories over the temptations the devil throws our way, openly and with such joy! Phone calls, emails, zoom meetings–technology has provided great ways to stay in touch, but there is nothing that can replace face to face interaction.

There is no doubt that the changes we have had to make have affected me. It's strange how God's timing works. I am retiring from the school system on August first. Prior to the shut-down, I was concerned about how I would deal with the transition from my crazy life as a behavior management technician. I was going from helping mentally and emotionally troubled teens, having my weeks planned out in advance so that I could ensure I'd accomplish all my required tasks, to the retired life of spending most of my days by myself, at home, creating art, or giving riding lessons. I knew that life was going to be really different. I knew that I was going to have to be disciplined in order to build my part-time freelance artist profession into a more full-time activity. But quarantine has nearly brought all of that to a screeching halt. I have had to remind myself frequently that God is in control of all of this. Proverbs 3:5-6 (NKJV) encourages me: "Trust in the Lord with all your heart and lean not on your own understanding, in all your ways acknowledge Him, and He shall direct your paths."

Lately, it seems like every time I look at social media or hear a message, Philippians 4:6 comes up:

> *Do not be anxious about* anything, *but in* everything *by* prayer *and* supplication *with* thanksgiving *let your requests be made known to God.*

Let's take note of a few of those emphasized words. *Prayer* is our form of communication with God. Prayer isn't just asking God for things. Prayer isn't just thanking God for things. Prayer is how we develop a relationship with Him. *Supplication* is the action of asking or begging for something earnestly and humbly, being "supple," flexible, and willing to bend–specifically, at the knees. We need to ask *with thanksgiving*. Thank Him for the blessings He so graciously gives and for answered prayer. This simple verse has so much direction that we can apply to our daily walk. It tells us what we should not do: "Do not be anxious," and then it tells us what we should do about anything and everything: pray, ask humbly, and be thankful.

I have been thinking about how my life had become so incredibly busy that I was really just going through the motions, just trying to keep up, constantly focused on the next task, and planning ahead, making sure that I had what I needed for upcoming events or tasks. Making sure

I had groceries to cook for church and home and time to do the cooking; making sure I had feed for horses, cats, dogs, and chickens and time to feed them; making sure that riding lessons, 4-H meetings, and church meetings were planned and organized. Constantly checking my calendar to make sure I hadn't forgotten anything had become my normal. Even putting a note to call my mom at least once a week was a necessity. Forget going to visit Mom and Dad–there was no time for that. There was no time to just "be still and know." No time to vary from the schedule. No time to listen to what God may want me to hear. No time for prayer, no time for supplication, and no time for thanksgiving.

My morning time of journaling and prayer had also become part of my daily schedule. But, again, I felt like I was only going through the motions. I ignored the still small voice that kept telling me to slow down, to take time to listen, and to give my burdens to Him. The Bible tells us to "cast all [our] anxiety on Him because He cares for [us]" (1 Peter 5:7, NIV). I attended many services where my heart felt like it was about to burst because the urge to go to that altar and lay it all down was overwhelming, but still I would not move. I refused. Pride, rebellious nature, and sin, got all in the way. I got in the way.

Things have changed now. Dramatically. With no school, no church services, and only a few riding lessons, the hustle and bustle exist no more. Something else changed too–my well-planned, well-organized life. My morning routine stopped, along with my journal and prayer time. I nearly quit journaling altogether for the first few weeks. I should now be praying and journaling more, not less. I should now spend more time seeking God, not less. Before I realized, I was slowly drifting away from God. I was still going to church and meeting with a few others, reading Scripture, and doing Bible studies, but that dedication was all in my head, not my heart, and I knew it. I even told my brothers about it. But I refused to do anything about it.

But God!

Everything changed on a typical Tuesday. Sometimes it takes something traumatic to shake me out of the catatonic stupor of living life, focusing on everything but God. And that is exactly what happened on Tuesday of this week.

A few days ago, I recommitted to journaling and praying every morning, asking God to forgive me for my nonchalant attitude toward Him. After my morning prayer time, I had to join a few online meetings. After the meetings, I decided to go ahead and complete an assignment, which entailed creating a video of me doing something I enjoy doing that helps me relax. The choice was a no-brainer. I would record myself riding my horse. However, I needed someone to video, so I called my daughter, Sadie.

I saddled my horse, Willow, and took her up to the pasture near the barn where the other horses would not bother us. My husband and I had just hung a new gate on the upper end of the barn with an electric strand of wire about eight inches above it to prevent the horses from putting their heads over and pushing on the gate. I took the electric strand down and swung the metal gate open, led my horse through, and let the gate swing shut. I mounted and rode around the pasture a little, waiting for my daughter. I rode up to the gate to get Willow close enough to swing it open. That is when my peaceful, relaxing day went awry.

The metal gate was now electrified due to the electric strand hanging down and touching the gate. Willow gently reached over with her nose, touching the electrified gate. Her world, too, got rocked, or I should say– shocked! She reacted exactly as a trainer would want from a horse to keep them safely inside a fence, but not as a rider would want while on her back. Willow wheeled left violently, where we then parted ways, landing me hard on my right elbow and shoulder.

Willow bolted, running laps around the pasture. I was able to slowly get up, catch my breath and my horse. I felt so bad for Willow, though, because she was terrified. After I let her settle, I was able to get back on and ride her long enough to get the video once Sadie arrived. To my relief, the spill was not captured on video.

After that adventure, I unsaddled, turned Willow out and then remembered that I needed to move the horses from one pasture to another for grazing. I was already getting stiff and sore, so I figured the walk would do me good. It was about a quarter mile to the gates that needed to be opened. My little dog, Chex, and Sadie's dog, Jake, walked with me. The horses were all standing at the gate, waiting on me, knowing they were going to greener pasture, literally. I opened the gate, letting them through. They took off, galloping hard up the hill. I normally love watching those beautiful creatures run, manes and tails streaming, stretching out, hooves pounding, free and uninhibited. But this day there was no joy as I turned to watch and saw Chex, laying seemingly lifeless, right in the direction that the horses took. Twice in one day, my world was rocked!

There was no slow movement on my part this time. I ran, falling to my knees, and picked that little dog up, sobbing and screaming, begging God, please no, not my sweet little dog! Supplication. How did that word come to my mind right at that moment? How did I think, in that dramatic, traumatic event, that it had been quite some time since I had been on my knees praying to my Father? Suddenly, that still small voice was all I heard over the terror in my own mind: "Come to me in prayer and supplication." I cradled that sweet dog in my arms and kissed his little face and prayed. I don't know how long I knelt there. It seemed like an eternity. In reality, it was probably only a brief moment before I felt a familiar lick on my face. I opened my eyes, thinking that I must be imagining, but no, it was my sweet little Chex. He was looking up at me as though he were asking, "What's wrong, mom?" Praise God! Talk about thanksgiving!

I held Chex, filled with relief and joy. Upon closer inspection, I noticed that he had been kicked. A small piece of hide was missing just above his eye. How it didn't kill him is a miracle. I carefully put him down to make sure he wasn't paralyzed. He was a little wobbly at first, but then he walked and followed me all the way home, right at my heels, close, instead of his usual rambling here and there. All the way home, I was thinking of that moment, on my knees. I don't know if I cried harder when I thought Chex was dead or when I realized he wasn't.
I continued to cry off and on that day, as well as into the next few days whenever I spoke about what happened or

even just thought of it. Those tears were tears of gratitude and thanksgiving. Psalm 28:6-7 (KJV) says, "Blessed be the Lord, because he hath heard the voice of my supplications. The Lord is my strength and my shield; my heart trusted in him, and I am helped: therefore, my heart greatly rejoiceth; and with my song will I praise Him." Yes! I hope that this day, one that could have ended tragically, will be a reminder, one that I will never forget, that prayer and supplication are important.

As I write this story, I continue to work from home and have decided to study how traumatic events change and rewire our brains. Many of the students that I work with have experienced trauma as young children. I have gone through training sessions that touch on what causes the changes in the brain, how to help those who have suffered trauma, and even how it can affect those who work with people who have suffered trauma. As I rehashed my training, I related it to God's Word and these events in my own life.

One great way to deal with trauma is to provide a safe, stable environment. The following Scriptures are just a few that show us what a loving, supportive, safe, and consistent heavenly Father we have if only we trust in Him:

The Lord is my shepherd; I shall not want.
(Psalm 23:1, KJV)

The Lord will rescue me from every evil deed, and will bring me safely to His heavenly Kingdom.
(2 Timothy 4:18, NASB)

SINGING IN THE DARK

Jesus Christ is the same yesterday and today and forever.
(Hebrews 13:8)

Every good thing given and every perfect gift is from above, coming down from the Father of lights, with whom there is no variation or shifting shadow.
(James 1:17)

Another very important step in the trauma survivor's healing process is to focus on the positive. Focus on the victory, not the victim. These verses speak powerfully of Christ's victory:

For whoever has been born of God overcomes the world; and this is the victory that has overcome the world: our faith.
(1 John 5:4)

But thanks be to God, who always leads us in triumph in Christ, and through us reveals the fragrance of the knowledge of Him in every place.
(2 Corinthians 2:14)

But in all these things we overwhelmingly conquer through Him who loved us.
(Romans 8:37)

Our victory is through Christ! Jesus was victimized, traumatized but was victorious overall even to death, so that we would not have to be victims. Through Him, and our faith in Him, we too are victors.

Additionally, those who help trauma victims stress the

importance of avoiding the use of alcohol and drugs. They must take care of themselves, eat a well-balanced diet, exercise, and try to stay physically healthy. The New Testament encourages believers to protect their bodies:

But I say, walk by the Spirit, and you will not carry out the desire of the flesh.
(Galatians 5:16)

If anyone destroys the temple of God, God will destroy that person; for the temple of God is holy, and that is what you are.
(1 Corinthians 3:17)

Or do you know not that your body is a temple of the Holy Spirit within you, whom you have from God, and that you are not your own, for you have been bought for a price: therefore glorify God in your body.
(1 Corinthians 6:19-20)

Therefore I urge you, brothers, by the mercies of God, to present your bodies as a living and holy sacrifice, acceptable to God, which is your spiritual service of worship. And do not be conformed to this world, but be transformed by the renewing of your mind, so that you may prove what the will of God is, that which is good and acceptable and perfect.
(Romans 12:1-2)

There are so many verses in Scripture to help those who have suffered trauma. But for those who do not believe the Bible, we as Christians can help them by showing Christ's love to them.

I endured a traumatic event as a young child. I have worked with school-age children for the last twenty-three years who have suffered from traumatic events in their young lives. Through all those experiences, I have come to a great realization. God gives us everything that we need, in His timing, in every situation. He loves me, and He is my safe place. He has given me His Word to seek guidance, and He has given me the perfect example of how to live through Christ Jesus, the Victor. He has provided me with some incredible people who have helped me and shown me His love. So, when we pray, when we are supple and willing to get on our knees, when we are humble, when we ask and are thankful and grateful for Him and all that He is and does, He will bless us, and He will give us what we need to help others. I still mess up, I still forget, and I still sin. But I know Him and He knows me. I hope that the more I mature, the less I will mess up, the less I will forget to turn to Him, and the less I will sin against Him.

The first event on that traumatic Tuesday could have ended much worse than it did. When I was lying flat on my back, I didn't think of God. I didn't immediately praise Him that I wasn't injured any worse, or better yet, killed. I went on with my day, stiff and sore, as though nothing had happened. That was exactly how I have been living my life lately. Going through life, crazy busy, ignoring God, thinking that I was doing good, doing His work, yet not thankful for all of His blessings and stiff and sore from not being supple and listening to Him.

Then, when my little dog was trampled, and I went to my knees, it shook me. It woke me up and made me realize that I have been behaving like a spoiled, ungrateful child.

SINGING IN THE DARK

Sometimes it takes a little trauma to shake us and make us turn to the One who protects, who heals, who loves when no one else will. The wounds of trauma can be healed if only we turn to Him.

Dear Lord, I will exalt You, my God the King; I will praise Your name for ever and ever. Great is the Lord and most worthy of praise; His greatness no one can fathom. Lord, I admit to You today that I have not been supple, I have not prayed to You as I should and I have not been thankful for the unending blessings You have given me. Forgive me when I fail You and fail to resist temptation. Help me to always remember that You are my Provider, my Keeper, my Safe place, my Redeemer and my Savior. Help me, Lord, to take care of this temple and help me resist temptation. God, I ask You today to keep me from evil, to keep my thoughts on You. I thank You for the brothers and sisters You have placed in my life, who love as You love and support and encourage not only me but all those they contact. Oh, what a blessing they are to me! But most of all, God, I thank You for Your Son Jesus Christ, the Victor over all, the one who came to claim victory over sin and death so I don't have to. Thank You for the sacrifice You made for all. I love You, Lord! Thank You for loving me. Amen.

SINGING IN THE DARK

Trail Horses

SINGING IN THE DARK

SINGING IN THE DARK

8/8/2020

Trail horses come in every shape, size, color, ability, and temperament imaginable. Trail riding is great for horses of every discipline, age, or maturity. It is good for the horses just beginning their training, known as 'green' horses, and just as beneficial for seasoned performance horses and even retired, older horses. Some horses go their entire lives being used for nothing but trail riding, and some may never see a trail, which is sad indeed. You just can't trail ride too much when it comes to the benefit of the horse. Trail riding does so much for a horse (and the rider).

I went for a short trail ride with a friend of mine today. I left my horse at home and rode one of his horses. The horse that he gave me to ride was new to me and fairly new to him. We weren't sure how she would behave on the trails, but she needed the experience, and we needed to know if she was trail savvy or not. My friend was riding a young, green gelding in training who wasn't a very confident trail horse, but he too needed the experience.

Before striking out, I tested the mare I was riding to see

how she responded to me–flexing her head and neck both ways with my hands and reins, checking for softness. She was incredibly soft to my hands. I barely touched the rein and she gave me her head quickly. Then I checked to see how she reacted to my legs and seat. Not so soft there. She did not move away from my leg when I pressed on her side and she did not slow down or stop when I sat deep in the saddle. This became much more obvious once we were in the woods.

We had to blaze a little because there was no trail in the beginning. In some places, the ground was soft and deep with stump holes and thick growth. The mare didn't pay much attention to where she was putting her feet, which is a characteristic I look for in a good trail horse. I believe this is a trait that comes with a lot of experience and something that can be developed over time. This caused me to work a little harder to help her avoid the holes and vines so that we didn't get tangled or tripped up. She would turn her head easily when I directed her with the slightest touch of the reins, but I needed her to move her whole body, feet included, to the left or right. I wanted her to move in response to my leg cues and step away from pressure to keep from bumping her shoulders and my knees into trees. She was so responsive to certain cues but not to others.

I learned another thing about this mare along the way. She was concerned with the horse my friend was riding out in front of her. This could have been the reason she wasn't paying attention to her footing. She would become a little anxious if the gelding got too far ahead of her. She would quicken her steps and rush a bit to catch up or try taking shortcuts, wanting to plow through whatever was between us. She lacked confidence in me as her leader because we didn't have a relationship. She didn't trust me. She didn't know me. Her natural instincts told her that safety was found with that other horse, not me. She had no idea, nor did it matter to her, that the horse in front of her was just as unsure of himself as she was. It only mattered that she be near him, since that was where she felt most secure.

I began relating this mare to myself as we rode along. How much of my life, my walk, has been so similar to this mare, right now. Even today, I have moments that I catch myself sharing the same characteristics: afraid, anxious, unsure. Uncertain of my footing, putting my focus on things in the world around me, seeking safety in the wrong people, places, or things. Lacking confidence in the One who really cares about me, whom I should be trusting to guide me always, especially when things get difficult. Sometimes I am quickly obedient to cues and then completely ignorant of others. I would be resistant, bumping into things or plowing through, getting tangled in snares or vines when anxiety struck.

I couldn't blame this mare for the trouble she was having. She just wasn't educated on the cues that I gave her. She had no idea that I wanted her to move away from the leg against her ribs. She didn't know that the change in my seat position was a direction to speed up, slow down, or relax. She had never been ridden on this land and I am not sure she'd been used much at all on trails. She had no idea what kind of leader I was. She didn't know if I cared about her well-being. Overall, she did well, considering all those factors. She was never blatantly defiant or disobedient. With a little training and experience she should become a nice trail horse.

My walk, too, has been a progressive thing, just as I think this mare's training has been and will continue to be. We should always be growing and learning in our faith. I believe that is what Paul meant when he said, "So then, my beloved, just as you have always obeyed, not as in my presence only, but now much more in my absence, work out your own salvation with fear and trembling" (Philippians 2:12).

The mare was very respectful to me; she wanted to please. In my relationship with God, "working out my salvation with fear and trembling" doesn't mean that I am constantly in fear of what will happen if I make mistakes, but about having a great respect for my Master. I should want to please Him. He created me, giving me the ultimate gift of eternal life. I know that He cares for me, so the least I can do is respect Him.

At times, I am plagued with a nagging question in my mind. With my dad's Alzheimer's diagnosis, the pandemic, the political and racial unrest in this country, my retirement and all the uncertainty that comes with it, I ask myself: In the world, in this life, on this side of eternity, what is the *one* thing I have that I couldn't stand to lose? I thought about my home, my material possessions, my horses, my beloved little dog, my family, friends and loved ones. I even thought about my salvation. My salvation is the one thing that I can rest assured, through God's Word and Jesus' sacrifice, I cannot lose.

Salvation is the gift of eternal life in Heaven. Yes, eternity forever and ever. God's Word, the Bible, tells me that if I want to live forever, I must believe in and trust God. John

17:3 says, "And this is eternal life, that they may know You, the only true God, and Jesus Christ whom you have sent." Romans 10:13 promises that "everyone who calls on the name of the Lord will be saved."

Those are promises! God doesn't go back on His word.

John 5:24 says, "Truly, truly, I say to you, the one who hears My word and believes Him who sent Me, has eternal life and does not come into judgment, but has passed out of death into life."

John 10: 28 says, "I give them eternal life, and they will never perish; and no one will snatch them out of my hand." God's Word assures me that I will be with Him when my life here is over, as Jesus says in John 14:1-3:

> *Do not let your heart be troubled; believe in God, believe also in Me. In My Father's house are many rooms; if that were not so, I would have told you, because I am going there to prepare a place for you. And if I go and prepare a place for you, I am coming again and will take you to myself, so that where I am, there you also will be.*

I don't worry about losing my salvation; I don't worry about losing my life.

After pondering those truths, I decided that the one thing I never want to lose is my relationship with God. My salvation is established. Just as that mare must work to respond to her trainers, my relationship with the Father requires more of my effort. The mare is a decent riding horse, and she will be able to be ridden as long as she is alive and healthy. However, she isn't what horse people would call 'finished.' When Jesus hung on that cross, dying, He said, "It is finished." That meant that His work was done. He did all there was to do to save all of mankind.

We now just have to accept that work. That's all. The mare, being unfinished, has more to do. She needs to accept that the person on her back is leading and teaching her. She has to learn that the rider is one who cares for her. The more obedient she is, the easier it will be to navigate through tough situations. I did not say that life would be easier. She has to learn to develop a relationship, one with trust and confidence in her master. She has to learn how to overcome the anxiety of her natural herd instincts by depending on the one who is in charge. She will learn these things through training and experience, being rewarded when she moves away from pressure.

Hebrews 11:6 says, "And without faith, it is impossible to please Him, for the one who comes to God must believe that He exists and that He proves to be One who rewards those who seek Him." Jesus did the work on the cross, now we must believe and seek Him for the reward. That mare, when she trusts the trainer, receives the reward: rest.

1 Peter 5:6-7 says, "Therefore humble yourselves under the mighty hand of God, so that He may exalt you at the proper time, having cast all your anxiety on Him, because He cares about you."

Once that horse learns to trust the trainer, her anxieties and her natural instincts will be much easier to resist. She will have humbled herself to the master. Before my relationship with the Master, I followed all the wrong parts of the world, other people, other things that felt good at the time. That mare wanted to follow the gelding in front of her, no matter what. Well, that was me, and I know that following can get a person in trouble! The Bible encourages believers to use discernment when choosing to follow another person's lead, as expressed in the following verses:

The righteous person is a guide to his neighbor, but the way of the wicked leads them astray.
(Proverbs 12:26)

Do not be mismatched with unbelievers; for what do righteousness and lawlessness share together or what does light have in common with darkness?
(2 Corinthians 6:14)

But flee from these things, you man of God, and pursue righteousness, godliness, faith, love, perseverance and gentleness.
(1 Timothy 6:11)

Today, when I consider the mess I made of things when following everything but God, I am oh so grateful for the relationship I have with Him now. I am so thankful for the people He has placed in my life who have helped me in my relationship with Him. I remember how I would get angry at those who would try to tell me that I shouldn't be hanging out with certain people, especially when I was a teenager. I refused to listen. Now, I am thankful for them. Hebrews 13:7 says,

Remember those who lead you, who spoke the word of

God to you; and considering the result of their way of life, imitate their faith.

I no longer follow just any old person who comes along and could lead me astray. I seek God's will, and I look for godliness. I inspect the fruit in their lives. I look and pay attention to the love they have for others.

Romans 6:16 says:

Do you know that the one to whom you present yourselves as slaves for obedience, you are slaves of that same one whom you obey, either of sin resulting in death, or of obedience resulting in righteousness.

That mare could choose to be obedient to her natural instincts and follow the gelding who could possibly lead her and her rider off a cliff to her doom, or she could choose obedience that will lead to her being the soft, supple servant all riders dream of owning. I am now more cautious of who I allow to lead me, as we all should be. We must "be of sober spirit, be on the alert" because our "adversary, the devil, prowls around like a roaring lion, seeking someone to devour" (1 Peter 5:8).

If I am not seeking His righteousness, His will in my life, and being obedient to Him, then I am a slave to sin. If I am not constantly working to build my relationship with Him, I can be easily led astray, falling into holes, and getting entangled in vines and snares.

Ephesians 2 summarizes my journey. The first verse says, "And you were dead in your offenses and sins, in which you previously walked according to the course of this world." I surely was.

The second verse continues to describe how we walked "according to the power of the prince of the air, of the spirit that is now working in the sons of disobedience." I was disobedient! I was following the devil.

Verse 3 says, "Among them we too all previously lived in the lusts of our flesh, indulging the desires of the flesh and of the mind, and were by nature children of wrath, just as the rest." I deserve nothing but God's wrath. What a wretched mess I was! "But God, being rich in mercy, because of His great love with which He loved us, even when we were dead in our wrongdoings, made us alive together with Christ (by grace you have been saved)" (Ephesians 2:4, emphasis added). Praise God! Hallelujah!

The chapter continues:

And raised us up with Him, and seated us with Him in the heavenly places in Christ Jesus, so that in the ages to come He might show the boundless riches of his grace in his kindness toward us in Christ Jesus. For by grace you have been saved through faith; and this is not from yourselves, it is the gift of God; not a result of works, so that no one may boast.

Remember, Jesus did all the work.

Verse 10 says, "For we are His workmanship, created in Christ Jesus for good works, which God prepared in beforehand so that we would walk in them." Our "good works" are obedience–the fruits of love, joy, peace, patience, kindness, goodness, faithfulness, gentleness, and self-control. We have the ability to be humble, shine the light of Jesus in a dark world, and help others to know and have a relationship with Him.

Verse 13 says, "But now in Christ Jesus you who previously were far away have been brought near by the blood of Christ." Like that nice mare, who still needs to learn more about what her master wants from her, I too am still learning and growing in my walk with the Lord. I hope to build on my relationship with Christ Jesus, the chief Cornerstone. I want to stand firm in my faith when obstacles come.

Finally verse 22 says that "in [Christ] you also are being built together into a dwelling of God in the Spirit." If I choose to spend time with people who are also working on their relationship with the Father, then we become the dwelling, the church, where God lives! Oh, this is my prayer!

Oh God, Master of all things, dwell in me. Live in me by your Holy Spirit. Please lead and guide me. Lead and guide those around me, my brothers and sisters. Draw us near to You. Help me, Master, to be soft to Your cues. Let me not be dull or ignorant to what You ask of me. Keep my focus on You, Lord, and get rid of the distractions of this world. Lord, I am a sinner. I forget to devote myself to our relationship at times. I wander off and let this flesh hinder my walk with You. Forgive me. I thank You for doing the work so I can rest in the finished sacrifice You gave. Thank You for the mercy and grace that You so graciously give daily. I love You, Lord. Amen.

Gates

SINGING IN THE DARK

SINGING IN THE DARK

7/24/2021

I have been having this thought about gates for a little bit.

Living on a farm for most of my life, I've found that gates are a really big deal, especially when you have animals, cattle, horses, pigs, even chickens or dogs. To keep those animals contained, you must have gates. Gates are the way to put more animals in and keep other things out. My husband recently put up a new gate at the back of our property that we cannot see from our house. There is access to the gate from the road, causing us some concern since we have found evidence of vehicles parking there and leaving garbage, empty alcohol bottles, and other litter. We fear that someone could open the gate, allowing the animals to escape, or even worse, stealing our animals. I recently saw a quite comical video of a little boy trying to close two swinging gates. He would push one side and then run to the other. By the time he had it, the other one had swung open again. Sometimes life feels that way to me–like I'm juggling too many things at once, not accomplishing anything. Running from one gate to the other just praying the cows don't get out!

SINGING IN THE DARK

When you ride horses and work with cattle, it's much easier to open and close gates if you teach your horse to walk up beside the gate and allow you to open and close it from their back. We have held obstacle clinics and challenges at Circle K Arena, my friend Darrell's ranch, where he trains horses and also where our church meets. It has become a very popular activity for horse riders. One of the obstacles we include is a gate. It may sound easy, but it can be a difficult challenge for an inexperienced horse or rider.

A few weeks ago, two friends and I decided that we were going to try our hand at a sorting cattle drive competition. The competition begins with three riders on horseback and a herd of cattle. The goal is to sort three of the cows out from the rest of the herd in a small pen, through a gate, and into an open arena. In the large arena, poles are set up so the riders have to drive the three steers into another small pen at the other end. The team with the fastest time wins. The herd was about eleven or twelve cows, visibly numbered. Each team is given three numbers matching the cows you have to sort out before entering the pen. The best way to sort cattle this way is to have one rider "hold" (not literally or physically) the gate by standing in the opening on their horse while the other riders separate the cows, usually one at a time unless you get lucky and your three cows are all together. When at least one of your numbered cows is headed towards the opening of the gate, the rider holding the gate has to get out of the way but also make sure none of the other cows try to go through. If a wrong-numbered cow gets through, you have to start over.

Cows are herd animals and feel safer in groups. When one cow goes through a gate it's usually much easier to get the rest through. Sometimes it can be very difficult to separate one cow and get it through a gate by itself.

After you get the three correctly numbered cows out into the open arena you are supposed to drive those three cows through the poles in a certain order around the arena. Getting those three cows to stay together and go through those poles can be very tricky. Turning them, keeping them from scattering and trying to run back to the pen where all the other cows are is quite a challenge.

Matthew 7:13-14 says, "Enter through the narrow gate; for the gate is wide and the way is broad that leads to destruction, and there are many who enter through it. For the gate is narrow and the way is constricted that leads to life, and there are few who find it."

What does Jesus mean when He says, "Wide is the gate and broad is the way that leads to destruction, and many enter through it"?

I picture a bunch of people walking down the road, doing wrong things, and at the end of the road is hell. They may not realize their destination. They are just going because everyone else is. That is where they are going: hell.

What does Jesus mean when He says, "The gate is narrow and the way is constricted that leads to life, and there are few who find it"?

He's saying that only some people, not most people, will believe in Jesus, do the right things, and go to Heaven when they die. Picture a couple of people walking down another road, doing the right things, and at the end of that road is Heaven.

Walking the narrow way can be hard when everyone else is walking the wide road. It's hard to be a Christian when other people aren't. It's hard to do the right things when other people do the wrong things. But we know that if we do walk the narrow way and believe in Jesus and do what He wants us to, then in the end, we'll get the reward of going to Heaven.

One thing that I have learned about working with cattle is that some cows are more likely to leave the herd than others. Those are the cows you want to draw first if you're in a sorting. They are much easier to separate and drive through the gate by themselves. Then there are others who really don't want to be alone at all. They will bolt through the gate if they feel like they are getting left behind or they will bunch up with the others, unwilling to get separated. Then when you start driving them through the poles, if you have three that are unwilling to separate, they are easier to drive because they want to stay close to the other two.

This herding concept can be a double-edged sword when applied to our walk of faith. We have to be careful of who is trying to separate us out from the herd, and who the herd is. If my herd mates are fellow Christians, believers in Jesus Christ, then I want to stay near them and not let Satan separate me out. However, if my herd is made up of non-believers, I must be willing to separate myself from them to walk through the narrow gate.

Besides being part of a city's protection against invaders, city gates were places of much activity in biblical times. At the city gates, business transactions were made, court was convened, and public announcements were given.

The Bible tells of "sitting in the gate" or in other words, the activities that took place at the gate. In Proverbs 1:21, wisdom is personified: "At the head of the noisy streets she cries out; At the entrance of the gates in the city she declares her sayings." To spread her words to the maximum number of people, Wisdom stands at the gates.

Ultimately, I want to follow Jesus wherever He leads me and have the knowledge and discernment to know His voice.

The first mention of a city gate is found in Genesis 19:1. Abraham's nephew, Lot, greeted the angelic visitors of his city at the gate of Sodom. Lot was there with other leading men of the city, discussing the day's issues and taking care of important business.

In the Law of Moses, parents of a rebellious son were told to bring him to the city gate, where the elders would examine the evidence and pass judgment (Deuteronomy 21:18-21). This shows that the city gate was important to community action.

Another important example is found in the book of Ruth. In Ruth 4:1-11, Boaz officially claimed the position of kinsman-redeemer by meeting with the city elders at the gate of Bethlehem. There, the legal matters regarding his marriage to Ruth were settled.

As Israel combated the Philistines, the priest Eli waited at the city gate for news about the ark and to hear how his sons fared in the battle (1 Samuel 4:18).

When King David ruled Israel, he stood before his troops to give instructions from the city gate (2 Samuel 18:1-

5). After his son Absalom died, David mourned but eventually returned to the city gate with his people (2 Samuel 19:1-8). The king's appearance at the gate signaled that the mourning was over, and the king was once again attending to the business of governing.

Esther 2:5-8 tells that some of the king's servants plotted at the king's gate to murder him. Mordecai, a leading Jew in Persia, heard the plot and reported it to Esther, who gave the news to the king (Esther 2:19-23). The Persian court officials were identified as being "at the king's gate" (3:3).

To control the gates of your enemies was to conquer their city. Part of Abraham's blessing from the Lord was the promise that "your seed shall possess the gate of their enemies" (Genesis 22:17).

When Jesus promised to build His Church, He said, "The gates of Hades will not overcome it" (Matthew 16:18). Since a gate was a place where rulers met and counsel was given, Jesus was saying that all the evil plans of Satan himself would never defeat the Church.

In Acts 3, the lame man was healed at the gate called Beautiful.

Psalm 147:13 says, "For He has strengthened the bars of your gates; He has blessed your sons within you."

Revelation 22:14 says, "Blessed are those who wash their robes, so that they may have the right to the tree of life, and may enter the city by the gates."

Revelation 21:25 says, "In the daytime (for there will be

no night there) its gates will never be closed."

I have found that in sorting cattle and in my walk of faith, guarding the gate is extremely important. How we take in information and process it is how things enter through the doors and gates of our soul. Our five senses are gates that allow information to enter our minds. Philippians 4:7 says, "And the peace of God, which surpasses all understanding, will guard your hearts and your minds in Christ Jesus."

The Bible tells us to "take every thought captive" (2 Corinthians 10:5, ESV). That means that I have a chance to do something about all thoughts that are not pleasing to God before they enter my heart and become a part of me. "As he thinks within himself, so he is" (Proverbs 23:7).

What we think about determines who we are.

We must guard our minds like that rider in the gate, allowing some thoughts through and blocking others.

The Bible shows us clearly in the Old Testament that the vulnerability and strength of a physical fortress always rested in its gates. This is the same in the spiritual fortress. The gates of the ancient cities are not like our gates today. They were massive and made of stone, iron, brass, or wood, and frequently sheeted with metal. They were tall and wide. "The Beautiful Gate" of Herod's temple (Acts 3:2) was made of brass and required twenty men to close it. These gates were opened during the day to allow the citizens to come and go but were generally closed and barred at night as a safety measure to keep out enemy attacks. Whoever controlled the gates of the stronghold ruled the city.

The gates were shut at nightfall (Joshua 2:5) because they were the chief point from which the enemy attacked (Judges 5:8). Idolatrous acts were performed at the gates (Acts 14:13). Battering rams were set against the gates (Ezekiel 21:22) and the gates were broken down and burned with fire (Nehemiah 1:3).

The gates were seats of authority (Ruth 4:11). At the gates, wisdom was uttered (Proverbs 1:21). Judges and officers served at the gates administering justice (Deuteronomy 16:18) and the councils of state were held at the gates (2 Chronicles 18:9). The Word was read (Nehemiah 8:2-3) and the prophets proclaimed God's message (Jeremiah 17:19-20) from the gates. The people also had to enter through the gates to worship the Lord.

In the Scriptures, gates are found not only in cities but also in camps, houses, temples, and palaces. We, as God's people, are called God's dwelling place. The human body is called a tent or temple for the Holy Spirit.

Many Scriptures speak about the gates. Gates are something that you enter through, physically and spiritually. Every person has gates to their spirit, soul, and body. The Word tells us that when we receive Jesus, we are sealed with the Holy Spirit. The gates to our spirit are closed when our spirit becomes a new creation.

Ephesians 4:30 says, "Do not grieve the Holy Spirit of God, by whom you were sealed for the day of redemption."

SINGING IN THE DARK

Praise God, for He is the protector of our spirit!

Our body and soul have gates that the enemy can and will attack. However, Jesus is our provision. He paid the price, taking the sins of the world for our redemption. He came to show mankind the way and provided us both access to God and the ability to walk in His power and victory. His sacrifice formed a gate so that we could enter into the kingdom of God. There is only one gate to reach the Father and that is through Jesus.

We must shut our open gates against the enemy. If even one gate is open and unprotected, we can fall prey to our enemy. God warns us not to give the devil a place. Gates of pride, rebellion, false beliefs, or wrong motives allow Satan to erect a fortress giving the enemy a place to establish his camp. We must keep watch over our gates. This means searching ourselves through the Holy Spirit and guarding the gates to our soul and body.

John 10:1-10 says:

> *"Truly, truly I say to you, the one who does not enter by the door into the fold of the sheep, but climbs up some other way, he is a thief and a robber. But the one who enters by the door is a shepherd of the sheep. To him the doorkeeper opens, and the sheep listens to his voice, and he calls his own sheep by name and leads them out. When he puts all his own sheep outside, he goes ahead of them, and the sheep follow him because they know his voice. However, a stranger they simply will not follow, but will flee from him, because they do not know the voice of strangers." Jesus told them this figure of speech, but they*

did not understand what the things which He was saying to them meant. So Jesus said to them again, "Truly, truly I say to you, I am the door of the sheep. All those who came before Me are thieves and robbers, but the sheep did not listen to them. I am the door; if anyone enters through Me, he will be saved, and will go in and out and find pasture. The thief comes only to steal and kill and destroy; I came so that they would have life, and have it abundantly."

I now have a greater respect for gates. I've always known the importance of gates from a physical perspective. But now, from a spiritual perspective, I will look at gates a little differently. When I make decisions in my walk, will I choose the easy way that may be wide and go along with many others through it? Or will I think twice, allowing my thoughts and steps to be led by The Shepherd?
Jesus said, "I am the gate."

I pray you choose Jesus. I pray you choose the way that is narrow and less used. I pray you enter the gate that is never closed. I pray it is guarded by the peace of God. I pray that your gate is strengthened by Him. I pray you tend to all of your business and take care of all your issues at the gate. I pray you possess the gate of your enemies. I pray you find healing at the gate. Amen!

SINGING IN THE DARK

Buddy Sour

SINGING IN THE DARK

SINGING IN THE DARK

2/21/2022

A horse that is "buddy sour" has separation anxiety. If the horse is taken away from his friend or his whole herd, and he can't see, hear, or smell them, then there is a good chance there could be trouble. This can be a dangerous problem if riders want to ride their horse away from its herd mates for any reason–whether it's trail riding alone, stopping to fix the tack, tighten the girth, pack the saddle bags, or taking a horse or two to the show ring. No matter the reason, separation will be a problem with a buddy sour horse. Any type of working or performance horse cannot have this vice and be successful. It just won't work. Buddy sour horses can display this aggravating vice by mildly pawing the ground or neighing. The horse with extreme anxiety can become dangerous for itself and/or its rider, rearing, lunging, spinning, bolting or bucking, doing whatever it takes to get back with those friends, back to comfort and safety.

Horses are herd animals and find protection in numbers. If a horse is less dominant, less confident, and untrained, then that horse may have a greater tendency to be buddy sour. The horse has an overwhelming natural instinct to be with other horses for safety. It can be incredibly difficult to convince a horse otherwise. Believe me, I know.

I once owned an absolutely beautiful palomino quarter horse gelding: well-bred, well-raised, and well-spoiled. He was the only foal I ever raised, and it showed. I failed him not only by letting him become buddy sour, but also he became fearful of horses he did not know after a traumatic experience. This created some very interesting situations on the trail, in the show ring, and in the roping pen. I came to understand at a later point in time that most of that gelding's issues were mine. I take full responsibility for my mistakes with that horse.

As Christians, we can be buddy sour. Anytime we put other relationships before God, The Master, we are buddy sour. The fear of being alone, the desires of the flesh, seeking attention, desiring acceptance, or craving emotional support from things of this world can cause us to be this way. Satan uses our weaknesses, our addictions, and our past, to make us think we need those things and that we can't survive without them. God uses our weaknesses to glorify Himself when we seek Him diligently, submit to Him, and allow Him to work through us, using His strength instead of our own. At some point, hopefully, sooner than later, we should come to know that *He* is *all* we really need.

One weekend, in June, my daughter, some friends, and I went on a trail riding and camping trip. After we arrived at the location, unloaded, and set up camp, several of us decided to go for a short ride. My daughter and her friend decided not to go, which meant her horse would be staying in the barn. My horse and my daughters horse pasture together all the time. So, I took my horse out to the hitching post and tied him there to groom and saddle him. He immediately began pawing and getting anxious. My daughter's horse, who was still up in the barn, whinnied. That was all it took.

That sweet, yellow horse of mine decided at that moment that he could no longer be without his herd-mate. He jumped over the hitching post while tied to it. He flipped, landing on his head. I thought he had broken his neck! The lead rope broke, and he jumped up, running on three legs as fast as he could to the barn to be with the one he felt he could not live without. He stood there by the mare in her stall, holding up his front right leg, refusing to put weight on it. I thought maybe he had broken his leg. But he was no longer anxious; he was with the one who brought him that sense of security.

I am not saying that we do not need our brothers and sisters in Christ. We do need those people in our lives for fellowship, encouragement, and support. We need them to hold us accountable when we begin to wander off the Lord's path. But we must be careful not to fall into the trap of allowing those relationships to become more important than our relationship with God. If separated from those people, we must be able to trust and rely on God to be our everything, especially during those times of loneliness or fearfulness.

During that trail riding trip, I spent the entire weekend in camp with my horse. His leg was swollen and painful, and there was no way I could ride him. I spent a lot of time hosing his leg and praying it wasn't something that was going to cause him to be lame the rest of his life or worse, that I would have to have him put down. I talked to God a lot that weekend. I remember the emotions: frustrated, sad, lonely, angry. Eventually, I was grateful, but it took a minute. My friends offered to stay in camp with me or to let me ride one of their horses. I didn't want them to miss out on the ride they had planned, so I insisted they go. It was not the trip I had planned, but I grew closer to God that weekend.

Undoubtedly, He knew that was what I needed. I did enjoy the peacefulness of the place and the time alone with Him. My horse's buddy sourness helped me work on mine.

Sometimes, Satan will do things to separate us from those who benefit us in our walk of faith in an attempt to also separate us from God. It's our choice how to handle those times. Sometimes, he will separate us from those who love us and then put others who truly don't in their place. The devil has no boundaries, and he will try every trick necessary to trip us up. We need to be able to discern who God places in our lives from those who are not for us.

Proverbs 12:26 says, "The righteous person is a guide to his neighbor, but the way of the wicked leads them astray."
That trick of separating us can happen at any time if we aren't paying attention. When we are young and green, we make new friends in school or work, and those friends become so important to us that we choose to do what they do, no matter the consequences. We get anxious or angry when someone who cares about us tells us that we shouldn't be hanging out with that person or doing those things.

It even happens to seasoned Christians. We meet someone from our past and decide to rekindle that relationship that really wasn't beneficial to us then, but maybe it was exciting and adventurous or made us feel good. Or we might meet someone who seems to have more financially, physically, and emotionally than we do, and we think we want that. We find ourselves getting attached to those worldly things or feelings, and the next thing you know, we feel like we can't live without it. It has become more important than God and the peace that comes from knowing Him. Or, we may think that we could hang out with someone in hopes of witnessing to them and influencing them, and soon find that we have picked up their bad habits or ways that are not pleasing to God. We must be careful.

Guard our heart at all times. Put on the full armor of God, always.

In 1 Corinthians 5:11, Paul says, "But actually I wrote to you not to associate with anyone so-called brother if he is a sexually immoral person, or greedy person, or an idolater, or is verbally abusive, or a swindler —not even to eat with such a person"

God's word does not mess around.

So how do we fix this vice of being buddy sour? We first need to develop a relationship with the horse. That's how trust starts. We don't just trust a perfect stranger and believe everything they tell us to be true. That takes time and experience. In the horse world, we call it groundwork. Then, we may get on and ride in a small area again, building that relationship and gaining trust. Eventually, we will work up to going out on the trail in a wide open space with obstacles to overcome. There are things along the trail that will test our faith. We may go out with a group of other riders and well-trained horses at first to build our confidence and go through those obstacles, following a seasoned horse. Then, as our trust builds, we may move to the head of the group, leading as we go. Eventually, hopefully, we learn to trust the Master enough to go out on our own, move on ahead of the group, or stay behind alone, if need be, without becoming anxious or fearful. We no longer need or depend on the herd for safety, but the Rider that we have learned to fully trust even in the most frightening, lonely circumstances.

Just beware! Even as a seasoned, well-trained, fully trusting Christian, there will be times when our faith may be thin. When the trail has been long and weary, when we are tired and want nothing more than to be at camp, resting with the herd. The load has been heavy for some time, and we begin to wonder if the Master truly has our best interest at heart. Our minds are tired. We forget to take every thought captive to the obedience of Jesus Christ our Lord and Savior (2 Corinthians 10:5). Along comes someone from the past, someone we knew (before Christ). Someone who knew us and knew our sins of the past. Trigger! There comes that slithering, sneaky, deceptive liar. The one who whispers, "You deserve a little fun." Or "It's pretty lonely out here on this trail all alone. You should have some company." Or "I am so afraid I can't do this alone!" Next thing you know, you are balking against your Master. You are kicking against the goads. You forgot what happened to Saul on the road to Damascus when Jesus told him that would hurt! You listen to the lies. You throw caution to the wind. It seems so much easier to do it this way, not His way!

Remember that gorgeous palomino gelding I spoke so highly of earlier? When we got home from the camping trip, he hopped off the trailer and ran on all four legs as though nothing had happened. My tried and true trail horse, ugh!

After thirteen years and many more mishaps, I sold my beloved horse to a great friend and brother. He took the horse that lacked confidence, that trembled in fear of other horses he didn't know, that would hurt someone in order to get his way, and he trained him to be confident in his job, either on the trail or in the rope pen. This trainer took time with him, lost his patience with him (and me as well, because he knew I created this mess), nearly killed him (not on purpose), but gave him a purpose, gained his trust and taught him how to pay attention and be obedient to him instead of focusing on all the things going on around him. By the way, this could have been a bad way to lose a brother. It's a good thing he is a very accomplished horseman and very forgiving of me!

My prayer is that you find brothers and sisters who you know and know you, who you can trust and love, and who share the love of the Father. Ask for God to give you those people who will pray for you to go through trials that will grow you closer to Him. Pray for those that if you get so far out there that you no longer hear the Holy Spirit or feel the conviction, they will encourage you, love you, pray for you, and help you in whatever way necessary, no matter what. I pray you will find those who bring you back into a place of repentance, where God's mercy and grace flow freely. Then you can find peace in knowing Jesus, your Redeemer, Lord, and Savior once again.

SINGING IN THE DARK

Oh God, you are an amazing Master! Your love, mercy, and grace are more than my pitiful mind can understand. The beauty of the trails You have led me down is unimaginable to so many. Lord, I fail You in so many ways. I have not always been trusting of You. I have gone off the path, and I tried my own way, my miserable way of understanding, too many times. I ask You, Father, today to lead me and guide me in Your way and always direct my path until my time here is over. Help me to choose wisely those with whom You would have me ride this trail. Protect me, protect my brothers and sisters from the wicked, sneaky ways of the devil that get sidetrack us so often. I thank You for never leaving or forsaking me when my rebellious spirit resists You and Your faithfulness. Thank You for Your soft and merciful hands. I thank You, Father, for the incredible buddies You have given me! I thank You for the struggles of riding buddy sour horses. I thank You for the trail guidance of the Holy Spirit and the map of Your Word. Thank You, Jesus, for loving me! Amen.

Singing in the Dark

SINGING IN THE DARK

SINGING IN THE DARK

4/21/2022

This morning, around 3:00 a.m., my little dog Chex woke me up so that he could go out as usual. I stumbled out of bed, took him out, and stepped out into the crisp, cool night air to the sound of a bird singing the most beautiful melody. I thought, *how strange*! The night was perfectly still and quiet except for this one bird singing loudly, or maybe it just seemed much louder because it was so dark and everything else was so quiet.

Chex came back in and we both crawled back in our beds. I lay there thinking about that bird. What kind of bird sings like that in the dark? After researching and listening to videos of songbirds of North Carolina, I found that it was a Northern Mockingbird.

Of course, I couldn't go back to sleep, so I prayed that God would reveal to me how this bird singing in the dark relates to me and my life. How amazing He is when we come to Him in the quiet stillness. I used to get frustrated waking up and not being able to go back to sleep, but when God reveals things to me in those times, I have come to cherish them immensely!

SINGING IN THE DARK

The Bible teaches us about darkness and light:

God saw that the light was good; and God separated the light from the darkness. God called the light "day" and the darkness he called "night." And there was evening, and there was morning, one day.
(Genesis 1:4-5)

The One forming light and creating darkness, causing well-being and creating disaster; I am the Lord who does all these things.
(Isaiah 45:7)

Lord, You have searched me. You know when I sit down and when I get up; You understand my thought from far away. You scrutinize my path and my lying down, and are acquainted with all my ways. Even before there is a word on my tongue, behold, Lord, You know it all. You have encircled me behind and in front, and placed Your hand upon me. Such knowledge is too wonderful for me; It is too high, I cannot comprehend it. Where can I go from Your Spirit? Or where can I flee from Your presence? If I ascend to heaven, You are there; If I make my bed in Sheol, behold, You are there. If I take up the wings of dawn, If I dwell in the remotest part of the sea, even there Your hand will lead me, And Your right hand will take hold of me. If I say, "Surely the darkness will overwhelm me, and the light around me will be night," Even darkness is not dark to You.
(Psalm 139:1-12)

I know darkness. I have made so many bad choices in my lifetime that put me in the dark. I have struggled with spiritual darkness many times, even recently, after thinking that all was right between me and God. After knowing the greatness of His light, I have learned that even when we think all is well, Satan can mess everything up if we are not diligently seeking God, constantly praying, fleeing temptation, and being obedient. If we let our guard down and begin looking for worldly things to help with our life problems such as stress, illnesses–whatever it is–the devil can twist evil to look good. When we make even one bad choice, we could find ourselves sitting in the dark.

My most recent experience with darkness stemmed from my anger towards God. The brain disease that has taken my earthly father, the man who helped me in my walk, the one I always turned to with spiritual questions, has left me angry, bitter, sad, and all the other emotions imaginable. I have been left not knowing how or what to pray for. I have felt so alone. Seeing the way that it has ravaged my sweet mom and broken her heart has been nearly unbearable at times. I have never felt so helpless in all of my life. It has been seven years of slowly, daily losing my dad. I have asked God, "Why?" a thousand times. I have been to the point of turning away from Him. I have been utterly exhausted in this whole situation, wanting to numb the pain in a bottle or any way that I thought might work.

John 11:10 says, "But if anyone walks during the night, he stumbles, because the light is not in him."

John 3:19-21 says,"And this is the judgment, that the light has come into the world, and people loved the darkness rather than the light; for their deeds were evil. For everyone who does evil hates the Light and does not come to the Light, so that his deeds will not be exposed. But the one who practices the truth comes to the Light, so that his deeds will be revealed as having been performed in God."

SINGING IN THE DARK

But God!

John 1:5 says, "And the light shines in the darkness and the darkness did not grasp it."

1 John 1:5-7 says, "This is the message we have heard from him and announce to you, that God is light, and in him is no darkness at all. If we say that we have fellowship with him and yet walk in darkness, we lie and do not practice the truth; but if we walk in the light, as he himself is in the light, we have fellowship with one another, and the blood of Jesus his Son cleanses us from all sin."

Psalm 27:1 says, "The Lord is my light and my salvation; whom should I fear? The Lord is the defense of my life; whom should I dread?"

I praise God in this moment of living in His light. I thank Him for pulling me out of the dark moments that I once chose over His light. I am ever grateful for the infinite mercy and grace that He has shown me.

Micah 7:8 says, "Do not rejoice over me, enemy of mine. Though I fall I will rise; Though I live in darkness, the Lord is a light for me."

I lay there in my bed, now much later than the original 3:00 a.m. awakening; I could *not* go back to sleep. I began thinking about my parents and all we have been through and still may have to endure. What a blessing it has been to have such wonderful parents. I am blessed to be able to care for them now. I thought of the seemingly endless night, reminding me of the story in Acts 16 about Paul and Silas.

SINGING IN THE DARK

On their way to the place of prayer, the apostles were met by a "slave woman who had a spirit of divination" (Acts 16:16). Her owner made a lot of money through her fortune-telling. Paul got annoyed with her because she followed them around for days, shouting, "These men are servants of the Most High God, who are telling you the way to be saved" (16:17). Aggravated, Paul said to the spirit, "I command you in the name of Jesus Christ to come out of her!" (16:18). And the spirit left her.

When her owners realized their money maker was gone, they "dragged [Paul and Silas] into the marketplace before the authorities" who had them arrested, beaten, shackled, and thrown into the deepest pits of the prison (16:19). Can you imagine what was going through the apostles' minds? They were obedient servants of our Lord, yet their freedom was taken away. They could have easily been resentful towards God. But they weren't. What did they do? Like the mockingbird in the cage, they sang! They prayed, and they praised their God.

The author of Acts writes:

> *Now about midnight Paul and Silas were praying and singing hymns of praise to God, and the prisoners were listening to them; and suddenly there was a great earthquake, so that the foundations of the prison were shaken; and immediately all the doors were opened, and everyone's chains were unfastened. When the jailer awoke and saw the prison doors opened, he drew his sword and was about to kill himself, thinking that the prisoners had escaped. But Paul called out with a loud voice, saying, "Do not harm yourself, for we are all here!" And the jailer asked for lights and rushed in, and trembling with fear, he*

SINGING IN THE DARK

fell down before Paul and Silas; and after he brought them out, he said, "Sirs, what must I do to be saved?" They said, "Believe in the Lord Jesus, and you will be saved, you and your household.
(Acts 16:25-31)

I know this message is for me! I am guilty of being in dark places, whether of my own accord or by God, and instead of glorifying and praising Him, I say, "Why God?" I get angry or resentful due to my pride. Instead of praying and praising Him, I put on a spirit of entitlement, believing I deserve better. I want so badly for this sinful flesh to turn to Him, to sing His praises so loudly that the earth shakes and His freedom comes to all those around me. I pray that He will use me and my brothers and sisters in faith to loose the chains that bind us and all those around us. That jailer and his entire family found God that very day!

Oh Lord, I come to you this day, tired but rejuvenated. Sleep eluded me last night, but You restored me! I praise You, my God, the Lord of all creation. The keeper of the mockingbirds that sing in the night. I am a wretched sinner who becomes a spoiled child when things get tough. I ask You, Lord, to help me. Help me to sing Your praises in the darkest of hours. Help me to turn from all the wickedness of this world and all the tricks of the devil and recognize you in the midst of darkness. Help me to bring the light of Jesus to all those around me. Thank you, God, for loving me even when I am so bad. Thank you for Your mercy and grace. Thank You for brothers and sisters who are willing to go through the darkness with me. Thank You for the mockingbird's song at 3:00 a.m. Thank you for the sleepless nights. Amen!

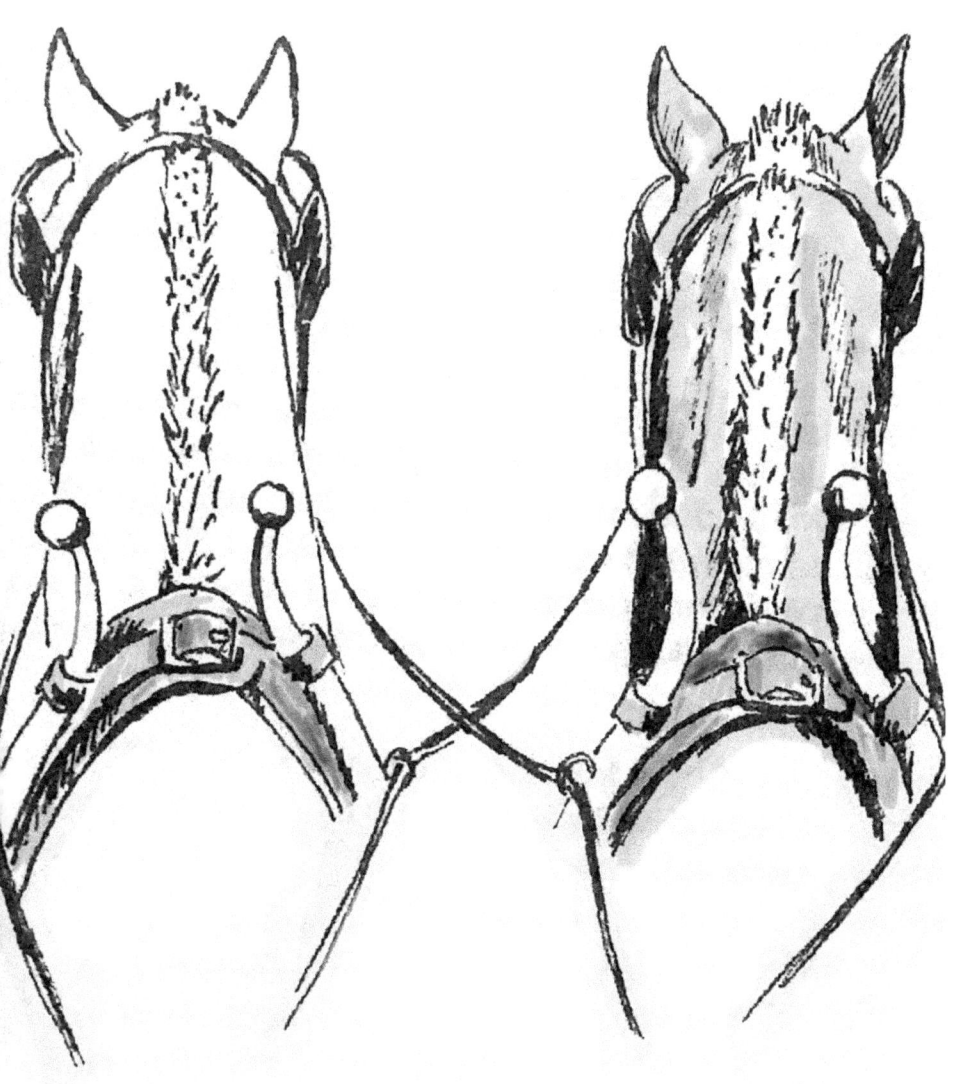

Friends

SINGING IN THE DARK

SINGING IN THE DARK

4/26/2023

Recently, I taught a Sunday School lesson for adults on John 17:14-19 which says:

I have given them Your word; and the world has hated them because they are not of the world, just as I am not of the world. I am not asking You to take them out of the world, but to keep them away from the evil one. They are not of the world, just as I am not of the world. Sanctify them in the truth; Your word is truth. Just as You sent Me into the world, I also sent them into the world. And for their sakes I sanctify Myself, so that they themselves also may be sanctified in truth.

We talked about being in the world but not of it, being spiritually insulated, and being equally yoked. This brought up some memories of my first job. When I was sixteen years old. I was hired at the Buffalo Ranch as a stagecoach driver. I was the youngest and one of two female drivers. However, I was determined to prove myself capable.

The Buffalo Ranch was the coolest place on earth as far as I was concerned. The ranch store was filled with clothing, boots, hats, tack and anything else a cowboy/cowgirl could possibly wish for. The smell of new leather would drown my senses as soon as I walked through those doors. Starry-eyed, I spent most of my earnings at that ranch store on things I thought I needed.

Yet, the best part was not inside the store. As I walked out the back, I was transported into another world, unlike any other experience on the East Coast. Stagecoaches waited to take guests down a dusty trail by a large lake through rolling fields where buffalo roamed alongside albino deer, antelope, longhorn, and watusi cattle.

After the stagecoach ride, the guests could walk up to the zoo which featured exotic animals including big cats, bears, monkeys, and giraffes. There was also a petting zoo with donkeys, zebras, ostriches and many other creatures great and small waiting for the cups of feed the visitors treated them to.

When I began working there, I thought I had the best job in the whole world. Sometimes, I still believe it was the best job I ever had. Was it an easy job? No! It was incredibly hard. Harnessing horses that stood much taller than me with harnesses that weighed half as much as me. Driving all day in the sweltering heat, dust filling every crevice and coating your sweat-covered skin, keeping the horses and yourself well hydrated between each run, cleaning harnesses, and feeding and grooming the horses before and after each long day was no easy task.

As a driver, my job was not only taking care of the animals that served us so well, but also knowing all there was to know about each of the animals in the park so I could answer the endless questions while also keeping the occupants of the stage safe. Some guests thought the animals in the park must be tame, leaving the stage to get closer pictures or, even better, to pet them! Then there were those who wanted to drive the stagecoach, or ride the horses, or hang out the windows, yelling for me to go faster around the hairpin turns or up and down the steep hills. At a young, impressionable age, I learned so much about people.

The horses also taught me a lot. I typically drove two different teams of two horses. Charlie and Friday were my favorite team. They were easy. Charlie was a stout, fairly tall, sorrel Appaloosa/Belgian cross gelding with a beautiful spotted rump. Friday was a Percheron cross, nearly the exact same height and build as Charlie, but a gorgeous gray. They both worked hard, but not overly so. They pulled straight with matching strides, pushing into the collar up the hills and sitting back in the harness going down. One would slow down if the other happened to stumble. Huge, humble, powerful gentlemen they were, never giving a minute's trouble.

Ecclesiastes 4:9-10, "Two are better than one because they have a good return for their labor; if either of them falls, one will lift up his companion. But woe to the one who falls when there is not another to lift him up!"

Then there was Doc and Sandy. Doc was a jet black, bulldog-built, massive Percheron cross gelding, and Sandy was just a bit smaller, sorrel, snowflake, Appaloosa/Belgian cross mare. Doc was the overachiever of them all while Sandy was the laziest. Doc would work until he fell dead if you asked him to. Sandy hated work and looked for every excuse not to. When we pulled out from the ranch store with a load of visitors, we came to a hill right away at the entrance of the park. Sandy would lay back and pull out to the right. Doc, bless his heart, pulled straight and hard, throwing himself into the collar, nearly pulling the load by himself and dragging Sandy along with him. I hated to, but usually, for the first few runs of the day, I would have to lay into Sandy with the driving whip until she got the idea that she wasn't going to get away with her laziness with me. Sometimes I would switch up the teams just to give Doc a break from Sandy.

I could not hook Charlie or Friday up with Sandy because if she decided she didn't want to work, they wouldn't drag her along like Doc did, so I would get the whip after her and then they would overreact to the whip and lunge forward, scared to death. That created a mess, with me trying to hold them back while simultaneously driving her forward. In contrast, Doc was so used to me using the whip on Sandy that he just ignored it and did his job as always.

Whenever I read 2 Corinthians 6:14 (NKJV), which commands Christians not to be mismatched or "unequally yoked with unbelievers," I think of how these horses– Doc, Charlie, and Friday–all worked well with one another. Doc could relax a bit when hitched with one of the other boys, but had to work extra hard to make up for Sandy's lack of effort when hitched with her. But Charlie and Friday would not work harder hitched with Sandy unless fear of the discipline dished out to her caused them to react. Charlie and Friday were the perfect team together, always steady and dependable. Their characteristics were as close to identical as any two horses could possibly be. Standing alone though, Doc was undeniably my favorite of the four, only because no matter which horse he was hitched with, he never changed. He worked hard, he had no fear but total respect for his driver, and he was most forgiving and most dependable. Then there was Sandy–lazy, afraid of everything, and unreliable with no respect for anything or anyone.

Although Doc was my favorite horse, Charlie and Friday were my favorite team. I loved them so much, mainly because of their unity. They were safe and reliable but, most importantly, they worked as one. I believe God feels the same way about us when we live in unity together. Psalm 133:1 says, "How good and how pleasant it is for brothers to live together in unity!"

One day, a man came to Buffalo Ranch to carve a huge tree at the top of a hill into the shape of a Native American statue. To the left of the road at the base of the hill was a sparkling lake. There, I had Doc and Sandy hitched to a loaded stagecoach. As I pulled them out from their hitching post and started up the hill, Sandy spotted the man at the top with his chainsaw, carving away at the tree. At that moment, halfway up the hill, Sandy froze. Spooking at this new thing up ahead, she started backing up. Fear had taken control of her mind. No amount of Doc lunging forward, no amount of driving-whip flailing, no screaming was stopping her.

As she backed up and Doc tried valiantly to pull forward, the stagecoach began to jack around with the backend going towards the lake banks. In that frantic moment,

I imagined what would happen in just a few more feet. I could envision the stagecoach dropping off the bank into the lake, taking the passengers, me, and these two horses with it. Just as I was about to jump down from my lofty perch, another driver saw what was happening and lunged for Sandy, pulling her forward at an angle where she couldn't see the woodcarver on top of the hill, just in time to keep us from plunging into the water.

Shaking and terrified, I unloaded the passengers, unhooked Sandy, and brought one of the more reliable team members down for the day. Later on I got Sandy back out and took her up to the top of the hill where the tree carver was, so that she could see there was no danger to her. I often wonder if she was truly afraid or if it was just a good excuse to get out of work!

The aforementioned passage in 2 Corinthians says,

> *Do not be mismatched with unbelievers; for what do righteousness and lawlessness share together, or what does light have in common with darkness? Or what harmony does Christ have with Belial, or what does a believer share with an unbeliever? Or what agreement does the temple of God have with idols? For we are the temple of the living God; just as God said, "I will dwell among them and walk among them; and I will be their God, and they shall be My people. Therefore, come out from their midst and be separate," says the Lord. "And do not touch what is unclean; and I will welcome you. And I will be a father to you, and you shall be sons and daughters to Me,"*
> *says the Lord Almighty.*
> (2 Corinthians 6:14-18)

Do you have friends who are lost in worldly things: fear, idols, addictions, sin of all sorts? Do you have friends who are strong in their faith, serving a mighty God with fear and trembling, who have an unwavering hope in the promises of His Word? I pray you do. I pray that you have more of the latter than the first. I pray that you are working out your salvation through Jesus Christ, along with other believers. I pray that you are grounded firmly enough in your faith that when you are with the friends who are backing up, nearly dropping off the bank, you may stand strong, overcome the fears of the flesh with the fear of God, and pull them out if you can. But whatever you do, do not allow them to drag you down along with them.

Charlie and Friday shared a special bond. Anytime I saw them outside of work, in their pasture with all the other horses, they were always close to one another. When they came in from pasture to the barn, the stall doors would be open for them to just choose a stall. Those two always came in together and went into stalls next to one another. If I ever chose to hitch one of them with Doc, the other would neigh and whinny. I do believe they loved each other in the capacity that horses can love. They served each other well. Yes, we can certainly learn a lot from them.

1 Peter 4:8-10 says, "Above all, keep fervent in your love for one another, because love covers a multitude of sins. Be hospitable to one another without complaint. As each one has received a special gift, employ it in serving one another as good stewards of the multifaceted grace of God."

Eventually, the owner of the ranch sold the land and the business. The new owners of the ranch had purchased a new team of horses. This team was young and inexperienced pulling a stagecoach, but they were beautiful, quicker, and lighter than the other teams. The older drivers tried to tell the owners that they should split this young team up, pairing them up with one of the older, heavier, more experienced horses until they could become accustomed to all that was there–the coach itself, the buffalo, the people. But the owners at that time knew little about horses and wanted these two, pretty, green, unpredictable creatures hooked to a rattling, top heavy, fully loaded coach on a busy weekend. It did not end well.

I was pulling out from the ranch with my coach loaded, when I looked and saw a young girl running down the hill screaming for help. I immediately jumped from my coach and secured my team to their tie post. Running up the hill, I saw a terrible sight. That beautiful team of horses was frantically lunging against their harness, trying to drag the stage which had flipped over on its side with the top popped open. People were tossed on the ground. The driver was trying to get up and over to the horses. I grabbed their heads and tried to calm them so we could get them unhooked from the wreckage. Two people broke their backs that day and several others sustained minor injuries. The driver of the coach later told us that the horses spooked from the sound of the rattling stage as they sped up to climb the hill near the back of the ranch. They bolted, jerking the lines from his hands and running out across the fields until the coach flipped over.

Little did I know at the time of this traumatic event that soon I too would be running wild, just as that team of horses, so afraid of the terrifying thing behind them, not knowing how to rid themselves of it other than to run hard and fast towards inevitable destruction instead of trusting the drivers hands. What a crazy, scary ride that was! But praise God, after quite a few years of that, I felt the tug of the line. And more importantly, I responded. I had run wild with wild friends long enough and knew that I needed something else before I ended up in a serious wreck.

The owners sold those two, inexperienced, unjustly treated horses and found replacements that were older and more experienced. Even then, they hooked those horses to an unloaded stagecoach with the old guys for their first few rides before expecting them to work like the seasoned teams, hauling loud and sometimes unruly passengers around a bunch of strange-smelling wild animals they'd never seen before.

1 Corinthians 15:33 says, "Do not be deceived: 'Bad company corrupts good morals.'"

It shames me to say that I did not appreciate all those horses at the Buffalo Ranch and the lessons I learned there until much later in my life. Charlie, Friday, Doc, and Sandy taught me so much. The boys taught me the value of good character; Sandy taught me just as much if not more. She taught me patience. She taught me to be firm but kind. She had her quirks and her character flaws and was much harder to get along with, but at the end of the day, she too was a great horse.

Lord Jesus, thank You for giving me such a vibrant community of friends to do life with. I praise You for the people you have blessed me with, the ones who have come alongside me to love, encourage, support, and uplift me through all the twists and turns of life. I'm so grateful that

I do not have to go through life alone, but that You have shown me examples of Your love through my dear friends. I pray that You would be present in my friendships, that You would be drawing us together in a deeper community toward greater unity with you. I pray that You would help heal any places of brokenness or discord in my friendships, and that You would restore any friendships that have fallen apart. I pray that for those friends who are lost, that You will help me be an example of Your love to them. Like Your Word says in Colossians 3:12-13, "So, as those who have been chosen of God, holy and beloved, put on a heart of compassion, kindness, humility, gentleness, and patience; bearing with one another, and forgiving each other, whoever has a complaint against anyone; just as the Lord forgave you, so must you do also." May I be patient with my friends, and may I forgive freely like You have forgiven me. May I shine Your light in my friendships, giving glory to You through all that I do, say, and think. In your name, I pray, Amen.

I would like to dedicate this story to *all* of my friends, those with whom I ran wild, those who have had to drag me along through my struggles, those whom I have had to drag, as well as those who have walked firmly and straight beside me. I love you all. Even better–God loves you too!

Tell God Your Plans

SINGING IN THE DARK

SINGING IN THE DARK

5/9/2023

Yesterday at our evening church service, the pastor preached from Romans 9. In that chapter, Paul says that he would be willing to give up his salvation in order for the people of Israel to know Christ as their Messiah.

Oh, to have that kind of longing for the lost!

Several years ago, the Lord really laid on my heart the urgency to do a street ministry in a small town near my home. Now, this wasn't just any town, at least not to me. My son's father (my ex) and all of his family live in this town. My relationship with my ex was not a healthy one. I was certainly not living for Jesus before, during, or even after those seven years I spent with him. The relationship was an abusive one. We both abused drugs and alcohol. The abuse was not something that I care to relive. I was traumatized, afraid to even drive through the town. Many years had passed. I had had very little contact with him or his family. I was no longer afraid, but the anxiety that I still felt when God so clearly directed my steps in that direction was something I struggled with.

Let me now explain what "street ministry" is. The Cowboy

Church that I attend started doing street ministry as a service to our local communities. We would plan by going out into a community, finding a place that would allow us to park horse trailers, and then setting a date to ride our horses through the community, praying with people and over the homes that we ride past. In my experience, this has been an awesome way to show the love of Christ to people who may have never seen or heard it. When people see horses coming down their street it opens the door for conversation that would not typically happen. Horses have a way of getting attention. God gave them to us, and we use them to glorify Him! A few times we have been able to set up in a neighborhood's central location where we serve food and lead people around on our horses, sharing Christ's love.

I had been praying about doing a street ministry, and God very clearly made it known to me that we were to go to this town, which triggered strong emotions, bad memories, and anxiety. At first, I said, "No way!" I wouldn't say anything about it to my brothers and sisters who would go to these events. The conviction was so strong it could not be ignored. I finally told my brother, our pastor, and he advised me not to ignore it. He knew the anxiety I felt. I also told one of my dearest lifelong friends who was there for me through those crazy years. She knew all that I had been through. Her husband is a pastor of another Cowboy Church that is located closer to the town than we were, so she too encouraged me to do what God was leading me to do. She talked to her husband, and they decided to join us. So, I half heartedly began planning the street ministry. I asked another of my brothers to go with me to this town to see if we could find a suitable place to park the horse trailers. He too knew my history and knew that this was not something I wanted to do alone–or at all.

Side-note, or where I'm from we say, "Squirrel!" Notice how loving and supportive my brothers and sisters are. Also notice, they encouraged obedience, knowing how difficult it was for me. Any one of them could have easily said, "No, I wouldn't do it" or encouraged me not to go. And they prayed. Those are good friends!

I was very selective about which side of town we were going to ride through, because the entire family lived on one side of the town, or so I thought. I had pulled up google maps, looked at the streets we were safe to go down, and prayed we could find a place to park on that side of the main street. As my brother and I drove down there, I prayed for God to make this easy, to go before us and open doors, open hearts. At the same time, I was praying that we would not run into that one particular person. Looking back now, I should have known better! How dare I wish to withhold God's love from anyone I had struggled to forgive. I had really struggled to learn how to pray for someone that I used to hate, someone who had threatened to kill me, someone who had threatened to take my child from me. The hurt ran deep and wide. But I am reminded that God's Word tells me to love my enemies. That's a tough one.

Matthew 5:43-48 says,

> *You have heard that it was said, "You shall love your neighbor and hate your enemy." But I say to you, love your enemies and pray for those who persecute you, so that you may prove yourselves to be sons of your Father who is in heaven. He causes His sun to rise on the evil and the good, and sends rain on the righteous. For if you love those who love you, what reward do you have? Even the*

tax collectors, do they not do the same? And if you greet only your brothers and sisters, what more are you doing than others? Even the Gentiles, do they not do the same? Therefore you shall be perfect, as your heavenly Father is perfect.

As we drove into the town, I had eyes only for the left side of the main street. Just a little way in, there was an abandoned service station with a large gravel lot behind it that would be perfect for parking our trailers. And, there was actually someone there about to walk in the front door of the building. We pulled in, and told the man what we were hoping to do. He quickly said, "Yes, that would be fine."

How much easier could it get? Thank you, Lord! I began to feel good about this adventure. I began to think that maybe this was going to work out perfectly. That we would be able to minister to a town that really needed it. That God was going to protect me from facing those old demons. Get in, get out, done! The plan was perfectly made.

Four of us were taking horses. My friend and her husband were taking a side-by-side to drive behind us and pick up the droppings from the horses. Several days after finding the perfect parking spot, my brother, his son, his son's best friend, and I loaded the horses. My friend and her husband loaded the John Deere gator, and we all headed out, praying before we left that God would have His way, keep us safe, and help us show His love.

What an incredible experience! We stopped and talked to many people. Many of those people were in great need. Many of them explained desperate and sad situations. My heart ached for them. We prayed with them. The Holy

SINGING IN THE DARK

Spirit was rushing around in His mighty windy way that day! How blessed we were.

As we were heading back to the trailer, I was elated! I was praising God for the incredible things He had done. I was thanking Him for keeping us safe. I was ever so grateful that I could take a deep breath. We were within maybe a hundred yards of the trailer. Only a few houses between us and that lovely parking place that He had so easily provided for us. It could not have gone any better!

We were riding along, the horses hooves clopping on pavement, laughing, chatting about what a wonderful day it had been. But then, I looked ahead. A few people were in their yard, grilling and enjoying the beautiful day. As we got closer all of the color drained from my face. No! It couldn't be. It wasn't possible. I turned to my brother, in shock, and then came the confirming whisper, "It's him." I turned to my friend behind us. She too had recognized him, and her jaw dropped in disbelief. All my careful planning was for nothing. Some people say, "If you want to hear God laugh, tell Him your plans." I know that He got a pretty good chuckle out of this.

I was riding a huge white gelding down the middle of a quiet little side street in hopes of gaining someone's attention so we could stop and speak with them. But at that moment, I wanted nothing more than to shrink away, to become invisible, to just poof–disappear. My heart was nearly bursting out of my chest, the reins sliding across sweaty palms, my head spinning. I pleaded, "Lord, please just let me stay on this horse! Don't let me fall off!"

As I internally spiraled, I heard a quiet whisper to my left: "It's gonna be okay," followed by a little chuckle and, "I was expecting horns and a pitchfork." As we got closer, the family recognized me and came to the edge of the road. The first words out of my ex's mouth made the hair stand up on the back of my neck. "Where's our boy?" he asked. The angry words I wanted to spew out was on the tip of my tongue. I swallowed and told him that our son didn't like riding horses. I then somehow managed to introduce everyone, explain what we were doing, and ask how they were. He told us that he was having some health issues and was going to the doctor for some tests. After some small talk, my brother asked if we could pray with them. I thought, *Surely he will say no.* He didn't. And we prayed.

In those moments, God freed me from so much that I had been holding for way too long. Even though I wasn't speaking the words of that prayer, my heart heard the words being spoken, and it broke apart.

Ezekiel 36:26 says, "Moreover, I will give you a new heart and put a new spirit within you; and I will remove the heart of stone from your flesh and give you a heart of flesh."

The healing washed over me like a cool summer shower after a long drought. I could feel the years of bitterness and hatred, the fear and the anxiety wisp away on the breeze of the Spirit. My senses were so elevated–going from the adrenaline rush of unexpectedly coming upon that family and the anger boiling up, to the elation that can only come from an almighty God. What a rush. If I had not been sitting on that horse, I don't think my feet would have been touching the ground anyway.

I went from saying, "God, how could You?" to "God, You are so good!" in a matter of moments. Only He can show us His goodness in the most unlikely places, you know. He orchestrated it all.

I thought I was doing what God wanted me to do for Him. How wrong I was. God was working all things for good. Romans 8:28 says, "And we know that God causes all things to work together for the good to those who love God, to those who are called according to His purpose." What an amazingly incredible God we have!

As we went on to the parking lot where we parked the horse trailers, I could barely talk. I don't even remember much of what took place afterward. I do remember that as we dismounted and began loading the horses into the trailers, his sister pulled up. My ex had called her and told her where I was. She was always so kind to me, and it had been a long time since I had last seen her. We talked and hugged and prayed with her as well. Since that reunion, she and I have kept in touch. She really seems to love the Lord.

What an awesome day!

Lord, You are amazing! You never cease to amaze me with Your works. Father, forgive me when I try to manipulate Your will to fit what I think is good for me. Forgive me for not completely trusting in You always in all things. God, I ask You today to give me a heart for You and a heart for your people. Help me to never withhold Your love from anyone, not even the ones who hurt me most. Lord, I long to love like You love. Thank You for the day on that street where You showed up and showed me how to forgive. Thank You for the healing that flooded my soul. Thank You for your mercy and grace. Amen.

SINGING IN THE DARK

Acknowledgements

There are many people to thank for their support, encouragement, prayers, and love during this endeavor, including those who walked by me through some of these stories. I'm just going to list them and hope that I haven't left anyone out. If I do leave someone out, God knows who you are and what you've done, which is truly what matters.

Thank you mom and dad. Thank you to my wonderful husband, Jamey Bost, who has put up with all of my shenanigans. Thank you to my children, Cody and Sadie. God bless you two! Thank you to all of my wonderful friends and brothers and sisters in Christ, Crystal, Melva, the HEARD, Hunter, and all of the faithful members of my closest body at Tri-County Cowboy Church, who were the first to hear these stories and pushed me to get them published. Thank you to my brother Darrell for your prayers, spiritual guidance, and patience along the way.

I would like to thank God above all for guiding my pen and giving me these words to share.

SINGING IN THE DARK

Deena Bost grew up and continues to live in the small town of Mt. Pleasant, North Carolina, where she was raised on a small farm alongside her brother. She and her husband now live on a farm just across town from where she grew up, where they raised their children and continue to enjoy farm life. Deena has been drawing since she was old enough to hold a pencil and pursued formal art training at Central Piedmont Community College. While commercial art was not the path she chose, her education prepared her for a successful career as a visual artist. She has completed numerous commissioned works and earned awards at local, regional, and national art shows. Deena spent 23 years working in the school system, using art to help students who struggled emotionally and behaviorally express themselves in healthy ways. After retiring, she felt the Lord leading her to focus fully on art and unexpectedly into the field of tattooing. She now owns an art gallery and tattoo studio, where she views her work as both creative expression and ministry. Deena teaches adult Sunday School and worships at Tri County Cowboy Church in Rockwell, North Carolina. Inspired by God's creation and His blessings, she writes from the heart and is grateful for the opportunity to share her gifts with others.

SINGING IN THE DARK

www.ingramcontent.com/pod-product-compliance
Lightning Source LLC
LaVergne TN
LVHW012038070526
838202LV00056B/5538